THE ELEMENTS OF TASTE

THE

ELEMENTS

OF

TASTE

GRAY KUNZ AND PETER KAMINSKY

PHOTOGRAPHS BY **ANDRÉ BARANOWSKI**
FOREWORD BY **BRYAN MILLER**

LITTLE, BROWN AND COMPANY
BOSTON NEW YORK LONDON

First Edition

Additional photography on pages 147 and 163 by Tom Aksters.

LIBRARY OF CONGRESS CATALOGING-IN-PUBLICATION DATA
Kunz, Gray.
    The elements of taste / by Gray Kunz and Peter Kaminsky;
photographs by André Baranowski; foreword by Bryan Miller—1st ed.
        p.   cm.
    Includes index.
    ISBN 0-316-60874-2
    1. Cookery.   2. Menus.   I. Kaminsky, Peter.   II. Title.

    TX651.K86 2001
641'.01'3 — dc21

                                                        2001029043

10   9   8   7   6   5   4   3   2   1

Imago

Design by Vertigo Design, NYC

PRINTED IN SINGAPORE

To Nicole, Julie, Jimmy, Melinda, Lucy, and Lily

"Almost all people are

born unconscious of

the nuances of flavour.

Many die so."

M.F.K. FISHER

FOREWORD

IN EARLY 1990 I MADE PLANS to dine at the sumptuous new dining room in the recently renovated Peninsula Hotel in midtown Manhattan. I didn't consider it an exciting prospect. In those years, hotel restaurants, for the most part, were rather perfunctory affairs that catered to road-weary hotel guests and distracted power-lunchers. As restaurant critic for the *New York Times*, however, I was compelled to check it out — fully expecting to flee after the first bite of dessert.

Surprisingly, though, the menu looked intriguing — then again, I had been ambushed by florid prose many times. At that time, so-called fusion cooking was not yet the gastronomic buzzword it is today, although a few chefs were experimenting with melding Asian ingredients with classic American and French cuisine. Yet this was the first menu I had seen that approached it with such passion and authority. To be honest, I don't recall every detail of that meal, but I clearly remember my first taste sensation. It was a dish of grilled jumbo shrimp set in a shallow, pellucid pool of shrimp stock. Yet the dish itself was infused with a flavor that was new to me, the kaffir lime. These bitter aromatic leaves defined and bolstered the sweetish broth, in the same way oak tannins frame a fine old Bordeaux.

Another startling creation, for both its flavor and texture, was a triple-decker of deboned quail that was layered with sweet taro-root chips and lustrous, perfectly seasoned creamed leeks. At the conclusion of this extraordinary meal I asked our captain for the name of the chef. Gray Kunz. Never heard of him.

I may not have known his name but I sure knew that this was the standard by which fusion cooking would soon be measured. After subsequently tasting the efforts of some other chefs, it was clear that one could not embrace this refined technique by cookbooks alone. The nuances of his Eastern flavors are revealed most subtly to those who have lived with them, as Gray had, from his childhood in Singapore.

In 1991 he moved to the St. Regis Hotel, literally across the street from the Peninsula, to take over its lavish restaurant, Lespinasse. For the first time I couldn't wait to get a reservation in a hotel dining room. The food at Lespinasse was even more spectacular. One dish that stood out was a Thai-influenced, steamed striped bass with fried shallots and minced lemon peel set over a heady broth redolent of citrus and mixed herbs. It was not long before chefs from around the country were excitedly queuing at his restaurant like kids at a carnival ride.

That same year I had the opportunity to observe Gray at work when he came out to East Hampton, Long Island, to cook with my longtime writing partner Pierre Franey, the renowned chef, *New York Times* columnist, and cookbook author. I was astounded at how Gray used ordinary supermarket ingredients to weave dishes that were amazingly simple yet with wonderfully stratified flavors that just kept washing over the palate. One nmight call it "contrapuntal cuisine," for its extraordinary balance and harmony.

Could I cook like this at home, or was this just too ethereal for even the skilled amateur? Another Gray admirer, food writer Peter Kaminsky, decided to give it a try. His idea was to deconstruct Gray's approach to food and, in the process, explain the principles behind great taste in a way that anyone could understand. The result is *The Elements of Taste*. Instead of writing a conventional cookbook that presents recipes as an end in themselves, Peter and Gray started by identifying the elemental flavors, and showed them at play in an array of Gray's signature dishes. In essence, they discovered the way great chefs think and gave it a language.

In a way, *The Elements of Taste* grabs the baton from Brillat-Savarin and carries it into the home kitchen. With this approach, recipes are guidelines, not dogma. Such a cooking strategy is akin to viewing a great painting in a museum: from ten feet away you can appreciate the overall image; from one foot away you savor the brilliance. *The Elements of Taste* is a different kind of cookbook, one that demands a degree of engagement from the reader. It also is original, thought-provoking, and savory — just like a four-star restaurant.

BRYAN MILLER

THE ELEMENTS OF TASTE

INTRODUCTION

CHEFS DON'T CREATE FROM RECIPES. They create from tastes. They create in the same way that a composer "hears" notes in the concert hall of the mind before anyone plays them on the keyboard. Kitchen artists draw on the knowledge acquired through years of study, long practice, and a generous dollop of intuition. If chefs are like composers in general, they are very like one composer in particular — Antonio Vivaldi. As a teacher in a foundling home for girls in Venice, his task each year was like that of a chef at the market: he could concoct his musical stew only with the materials at hand. If his star students played flute, oboe, and bassoon, he would write a piece for what was then an unusual combination of instruments. If the young ladies were more adept at guitar, he would dash off a slew of guitar pieces. Presumably if there had been a powerhouse conga drummer in the class, his oeuvre would certainly have included a concerto for harpsichord, lute, and conga.

Chefs work the same way: they start with the best of what is available and then turn to their intuition and their memories to figure out what might be done with those ingredients. A recipe may spring from a survey of the pantry, a trip to the refrigerator, a walk through the market, the memory of the smell of bacon on Sunday morning or of sage after a morning rain. As any fan of Hemingway or Proust knows, taste memories are among our strongest and most evocative. It was the memory of the taste of one little madeleine dissolved in a cup of tea that sent Proust careening through the next three thousand pages of remembrances. Had his memory been jogged by a complex dish like a bouillabaisse, he might have written his way through another foot or two of our bookshelves.

Like Proust's evocative memories, a chef's memories of taste lie at the base of any new recipe. You have a taste in your mind, an idea that it would go well cooked in a certain way or combined with a certain herb. Then you try that idea. You add ingredients and seasonings, reduced pan juices, maybe some lemon juice or wine, honey or sugar. Like a composer, you look for themes, motifs, and — most important — harmonies.

So, while this book contains recipes that you may cook as confidently as a musician can play through a score, it attempts something more important to the aspiring chef. It presents the thought process behind recipes, for that is how a chef creates. It always comes down to taste.

But what is taste?

Any food and wine fancier who keeps up on the current literature will have noticed that there are hundreds of volumes devoted to describing the experience of taste as it applies to just one food product . . . wine. There is a deep, rich (at times over-rich) vocabulary to turn to in order to understand and describe the experience of tasting a particular wine. It is a different case entirely for us beefeaters, burger kings, dairy queens, and cookie monsters.

For the tens of thousands of foodstuffs that are not wine, the vocabulary is limited and rudimentary. Restaurant critics describe food as "salty," "sweet," "smoky," "briny," "woodsy": all very general words that are often tossed in because the desperate reviewer has to say *something*. Pre-Renaissance scientists, in a similar quandary, described the world as being composed of earth, air, fire, and water. In taste as in science, we should have learned a few things since Galileo and the Borgias.

Having searched libraries and pointed and clicked our way through countless Internet pages, we found there is very little that has been written about taste. What we did find bears as much resemblance to the sensual experience of tasting as an anatomy textbook does to the *Kama Sutra*. Inevitably there is a listing of five taste receptors on the tongue, accompanied by line drawings as mouthwatering as a ball-bearing catalogue. Anyone who has ever made love (or a good pot roast) knows there is a lot more going on here than a few synapses firing off.

Though eating and loving are basic drives common to all creatures, true understanding of them requires more than instinct. Without that kind of understanding, today's ardent suitor becomes tomorrow's artless groper and the budding chef or gourmet is thrown

back on a jumble of trial-and-error experiences and slavish attempts to re-create a recipe in a book. A recipe is followed not because the reader understands everything that's going on in every step, but simply because it has a catchy title and some "expert" wrote it down in a cookbook.

All of us have, at one time or another, salivated over a picture in a cookbook and, by dint of hard work and following the directions to a *T,* turned out something just a cut above a braised running shoe. Following a recipe by rote requires little more than an ability to fill a measuring cup and read your watch. A cookbook is only a roadmap. It doesn't tell you if the ingredients in your local market are trucked in. Are the strawberries sweet or tart this year? Was the hog fed on apples or acorns? Was the fish frozen or is it fresh off the boat? All of these qualities influence taste, and they change from place to place, week to week, year to year.

This is not the way that a real chef works in the real world. The accomplished chef understands how taste works, what its components are, how it can be layered, how it must be balanced, and so on. This book is, we hope, a step toward a new way of understanding cuisine. It is a method and a vocabulary of taste that we have devised for the simple reason that there isn't another one to be had. We have refined it as we cooked and tasted and debated our way through each dish, but if we have been at all successful, it is our hope and expectation that the method itself will be refined by us and by others as time goes by.

Given a lack of literature about taste, we sat down and tasted. We ate apples, anchovies, pomegranates, prosciutto, morels, turnips, tarragon, Ben and Jerry's chocolate chip ice cream, Middle Eastern zatar, pizza, Vietnamese fish rolls, green tomatoes, passion fruit, venison, pickled papaya, cream of wheat, white truffles, black beans, red peppers, white chocolate, duck breast, frog legs, chicken wings, veal feet, beef cheeks . . . enough food to have sent Gargantua and Pantagruel from the table with tummyaches.

We had two goals, both of them equally important: the first, to devise a system that includes most of the tastes in the modern palate; the second, to simplify this system so that we didn't end up with so many tastes that we confused more than we explained. There is already a model for this approach in the wine world — component tasting. Although we have poked fun at this practice when taken to the extreme, the fact remains that good wine teachers actually do teach you how to break wine down into component tastes and, in so doing, to understand it more fully.

We have come up with fourteen basic tastes. Along the way, we sometimes had as many as twenty-two tastes, but that became rather unwieldy. We hated to let go of any and we debated over each of them as if we were the pledge committee at a fraternity considering a bumper crop of wonderful candidates. In the end, though, simplicity and our desire to create a reasonably practical book won out.

TASTES THAT PUSH

Not surprisingly, we started with some of the traditional basic tastes that we have all grown up knowing: salty, sweet, and hot. To avoid confusion between hot — as in spicy hot — and hot — as in burn-your-mouth hot — we chose the word "picante" to indicate the spicy heat of the chili pepper. These three tastes all share a basic characteristic: they heighten all the other tastes in a recipe. Like a wave approaching shore or a wind blowing across the plains, they push everything forward. Remove any of these tastes, and an interesting dish becomes dull and flaccid. Filet mignon becomes warm dead cow, ice cream becomes cold milk, chili becomes beans boiled in water. They are the foundation tastes, the fundamental chords in the melody of a meal. They also share one other quality: all three can be combined in the same recipe. In fact when chefs talk about "balancing a sauce" (and they all do), that normally means they're going to add some sugar (sweet), or salt, or pepper (picante). They also will balance with a fourth taste, tangy, but more about that later. For now, let us begin with the trinity of pushing tastes.

Salty

Salt is the king of tastes. This probably has something to do with all life coming from the sea. We require salt to keep the body functioning, but once life traded in its gills for lungs and took up residence on dry land, salt was not that common. We seek it out. Although modern humans can usually count on a reliable supply of salt, we still crave it the way our Neanderthal ancestors did on the Ice Age tundra. With supermarket aisles full of potato chips and salted nuts, it has been estimated that we probably consume 12,000 times more salt than our Paleolithic forebears. Salt, whether we get it from table salt, soy sauce, bacon, or Nacho Cheese Doritos, wakes up the other tastes.

Sweet

All human beings are born with a sweet tooth . . . with good reason. Sugar is an efficient fuel. It is found in highly nutritious foods, particularly fruits, which were easy for our savanna-dwelling forebears to gather (in season). In addition to being fine foods, oranges and bananas weren't as likely to trample you, or gore you with their horns, the way equally delicious meat on the hoof might. Sugar will often be the first taste to hit the palate. Just as often, it will have a tendency to move more toward the background of the overall taste and to round out the sharp edges of aromatic spices like cloves or very tangy lemon, and so forth. We had considered including fruity as a separate taste, but on closer consideration it seemed more accurate to say that fruity is a compound taste in the way that purple is a compound color, a combination of red and blue. Fruit, to be sure, is sweet and therefore pushes other tastes, but it also has a tangy component and a floral bouquet.

Picante

Peppery heat does have nerve endings on the tongue just like sweet, sour, salty, and bitter, but they're not taste buds per se. They are pain receptors, and they send out the same signals that are sent in response to heat from a flame, but as racy novelists have long known, pleasure and pain are linked opposites. Even if science does not recognize picante as a taste, try and tell that to a chef in Lima, Peru, or Lafayette, Louisiana. A simple dish like Cajun court bouillon calls for fish fillets, salt, pepper, tomatoes, and plenty of cayenne. Take away the cayenne, and it tastes like hospital food. On the other hand, a dose of peppery heat pushes forward every iota of taste potential in this simple but elegant combination.

TASTES THAT PULL

Where the "push" tastes have a tendency to put their shoulder into it and push all taste forward, the "pull" tastes seek out underlying flavors and highlight them. Some ingredients, like cooked onions or lemon juice, pull broadly, bringing every flavor forward. Others, like cinnamon or tarragon, are experienced as aromas that help to focus and highlight particular tastes. This brings us conveniently to the subject of the nose and smell. Brillat-Savarin, who thought more (and more clearly) about taste than anyone before or since, wrote "smell and taste form a single sense, of which the mouth is the laboratory and the nose is the chimney; or to speak more exactly, of which one serves for the tasting of actual body, the other for the savoring of their gases." Even though gas, as a term of culinary art, has fallen out of favor and, in fact, is downright indelicate, Brillat-Savarin had it exactly right. Without the nose, there is very little taste and there would certainly be no cuisine to speak of. Not every pull taste is sensed primarily in the nose, though. In fact, two of the most important ones are anchored on the palate.

Tangy

Tangy (often called sour) and its close cousin, the vinted taste of wine, are primarily experienced in the mouth rather than the nose. We say they pull rather than push because that is what it feels like. Think about it: when you have a lot of vinegar in something, the tongue feels as if it's contracting. Anyone who was ever puckered after biting into a tart lemon and then tasted a fried shrimp understands that the lemon feels as if it's pulling flavor out of the shrimp. In contrast to the push tastes, tangy ingredients never smooth out or round flavors: instead, they seem to brighten them and make them more distinct. If salt is the king of tastes, tangy is the queen, perhaps not the most faithful of queens, though: she partners up just as easily with sweet, hot, and just about every other taste with the possible exception of bitter.

Vinted

Had we undertaken to write this book about the tastes of the cuisines of China, India, Korea, Nigeria, or Morocco, we might well have forgone the taste of wine when used as an ingredient. Still, there's no question that in modern Western gastronomy wine is a critical element. Wine has an alchemistic capacity to elevate the tasting and dining experience. Enough has been written on wine as a beverage that we don't need to add our two cents. Our interest is in wine as a food ingredient. Wine has two pulling characteristics. As a fermented fruit, it has tang just like any other fruit, but it is rather more concentrated. Red wine, because of bitter tannins, "puckers" the tongue and makes it pull out even more flavor or taste. This bitterness helps wine to cut through other tastes and to clean the palate. The fruitiness in wine also pulls forward sweetness and complements salt. It is a powerful and complex ingredient and certainly a fundamental one in Western cuisine.

Bulby

The reason that so many recipes start with the instruction to "sweat shallots in oil" (or with the variation to brown some onions or garlic) is that it works so well. When you walk up to a house where someone is frying onions, you can tell before you even open the door what's going on inside. The same goes for a pan full of garlic, shallots, or leeks. They are all very forward aromas that tend to fill up the nose.

Clearly, these ingredients all have something in common, and just as clearly there isn't a common name for that common thing. We chose the word "bulby" for the reason that these members of the onion family all grow from bulbs, and it is the flesh of these sharp-tasting bulbs that is transformed by heat into one of the most effective carriers and enhancers of taste.

When eaten raw, bulby vegetables are odiferous, with a taste that some find pleasantly sharp but an aroma most considerately enjoyed at some distance from an intimate friend. Cooked bulby vegetables, however, are a sweetly different story. When you put them in a hot pan, bulby vegetables caramelize: their sharpness turns to nutty sugar. They are often the first aroma that arises from any dish. They have a pleasant sweetness, and as they fill up the nose with their bouquet, they have a tendency to pull all the flavors in a dish forward. They have a particular affinity for the sweet elements in meats and vegetables. In spite of this they don't pair up too well with some inherently sweet things like fruits. Of all the tastes that affect the nose and pull other tastes up, bulby ingredients do it most broadly.

Floral Herbal

Floral herbal ingredients are, for the most part, green and leafy but they also include such things as lemongrass and, for certain purposes, lemon zest or ginger. We call them floral because they remind us of flowers and their delicate aromas. They often serve to pull up and focus specific tastes. Thus, the herbs that have a licoricey taste, such as tarragon and basil, will pull up the sweet side of a recipe. Rosemary, thyme, and oregano accent saltiness, meatiness, and fishiness, as well as helping to define the garden tastes of tomato, peppers, and so on. Chili peppers and cilantro go together so well that in Mexican cooking it is hard to find picante tastes without cilantro alongside. Lemon zest and ginger accent the element in fruit that differentiates it from pure sugar.

In context, some other ingredients can serve a floral herbal function from time to time. Olive oil has a floral aspect that works well with herbs and makes it superior to other oils or butter when you want to bring out the garden vegetable side of things. Likewise, honey adds a floral note to sweetness that sets it apart from cane sugar or maple syrup. We use the word *floral* metaphorically, but it can also be taken literally. For example New Delhi chefs bathe some desserts in rosewater, and the Zapotecs of Oaxaca, Mexico, make a memorable quail with rose petals.

Spiced Aromatic

If we return to our musical analogy, floral herbs discussed above are like a harp or chimes — maybe even a piccolo: they are there as ornament and accent, delicate as lace, brittle as rime ice. The ingredients that we think of as spiced aromatic — such as cinnamon, cloves, allspice, mace, coriander seed, cumin, saffron, star anise — bring to mind trumpets and flutes: they rise over the rest of the ensemble, their notes ring out clearly and identifiably, restating themes and signaling new ones.

When experienced as pure taste on the tongue, these ingredients are often bitter, but their function is not so much mouth taste as it is the aroma that pulls up taste. Their bouquet rises clearly and identifiably out of the most complex mix of ingredients. They will pull up sweetness and temper it — think of cinnamon or allspice in cookies. Curry will bring out the subtle oceanic tones in shellfish. Cloves will focus the roundness of pork. Coriander seed and black pepper serve as messengers heralding the approach of substantial meaty tastes.

Spiced aromatic ingredients can also work to enhance the bouquet of other pulling ingredients — for example, curry pairs up nicely with lemongrass. Of course there's always the question of context. In music, a solo instrument serves a different purpose than the same instrument in a chamber group or orchestra. In much the same way, a spice rub on the outside of a pork roast immediately sets up the meaty taste, while the same spices cooked into a sauce will come later in the overall melody of the recipe. A word of caution: don't be misled into thinking that the more weird spices you add, the closer you will get to being a gourmet chef. There are more combinations that don't work out than there are ones that do. Prime chef directive: if it doesn't add then it detracts.

Funky

In this group, we include cabbage, truffles, aged meats like country ham, and cheeses, especially pungent cheeses. This is a category name that was a bit of a struggle. Clearly we are talking about a wide group of ingredients that are different in every respect except one: they are, for want of a better term, "stinky." While that may be the most accurate term, who wants to cook their way through a book with instructions like "take a nice stinky cheese and melt it over some cabbage that has been braised until it smells like the inside of a running shoe."

Still, there is no denying that these ingredients all have an organic, overripe smell that is, well, funky. A pig or a truffle hound does not dig through the earth for truffles because they are an expensive delicacy. To a pig or a hound (and, to be scientifically accurate, to us humans as well), a truffle has the scent of a willing mate.

The smell and taste of aged, highly organic ingredients stimulates the palate and pulls up strong flavors. Truffles with beef will accent the meatiness of the animal (and all animals have a slight gaminess to their flesh). A twenty-two-month-old country ham from Kentucky will have complex layers of taste that no fresh pork can rival. It will enhance recipes in the way great wine will do things that are far beyond the power of simple grape juice. While other ingredients such as fresh herbs and ground spices pull tastes up into more defined and ethereal areas of flavor, funky ingredients pull all of them back into their basic organic origins. It's that same primal tension between base matter and lofty spirituality that makes us human, so why wouldn't it work in food?

TASTE PLATFORMS

Vegetables, meat, fish, and poultry are most often thought of as the foundation elements — the platforms — upon which we build recipes. After all, you don't very often see recipes such as "Pan-Roasted Clove Bits Garnished with Saddle of Lamb" or "Rosemary Sprigs Sprinkled with Yellow Tomato Coulis." Common sense, or at least common practice, makes the vegetable, meat, fish, or poultry the centerpiece in naming a recipe. As you will see by cooking your way through this book, this is not the way we come up with recipes. Just as often we will start from the scent of an herb, the pungency of a spice, the heady perfume of a forest mushroom, the idea of combining hot and cold or smooth and crisp. With that as a starting point, we will begin to add ingredients and tastes. We think of vegetables and flesh not so much as "main ingredients" (although at times they certainly are); it is more accurate to call them platforms upon which other tastes can stand and interact.

All platform ingredients have a textural element, which is a key, though often overlooked, component in the whole taste process. Your mouth seeks texture before it begins to define tastes. If something is crunchy, you will always notice the crunch first: it punctuates one set of tastes and begins another. If something is creamy or smooth, it will round out tastes, meld them, and help tone down sharp edges. If something is toothy, like a piece of meat, what happens is you bite down and, as you do, you breathe out, releasing all the aroma components into the nose, thus pulling up flavor.

Like a well-behaved child in grade school, platform ingredients "work well with others," and like a well-adjusted child (or grown-up for that matter) they also have strong personalities of their own.

Garden

We were sitting in the Kunz kitchen in the Hudson Valley on a very hot August afternoon. We fled the kitchen for a walk in the garden, where we picked some zucchini and tomatoes. We sliced the zucchinis and tasted them: there's nothing like a fresh vegetable still warm from the sun at its peak of ripeness. Equally succulent was the beefsteak tomato that bulged and rippled in a way that no hothouse or agribusiness tomato ever does.

A tomato certainly has a different taste from a zucchini. Similarly, bell peppers, snap peas, romaine lettuce, and string beans all look different and have distinctive tastes of their own, but they all bring some common elements to a recipe. First, they all have a refreshing watery aspect. When eaten raw or lightly cooked, they have a pleasing crunch. In comparison to flesh or starches, there's a brightness to them that stops just short of tanginess. They also have some sugar, which sweetens and smoothes and allows us to caramelize them, thereby intensifying other flavors. We grow these things in a garden, so we call this taste, quite straightforwardly, Garden Vegetable.

Meaty

All ingredients and tastes are equal, but for many of us meat is the main ingredient. There really are few aromas more tantalizing than meat on the fire or few feelings more satisfying than biting down on a mouthful of cooked meat. Meat is hard to overpower with other ingredients, and it can support, accommodate, and improve spices, herbs, wine, vinegar, breading, and brining. Having said all that, it may surprise you when we assert that mouth flavor is not the primary taste characteristic of meat. Sure, we can all taste the difference between lamb and pork, beef and goose (we include poultry in the meat category), but that is not because meat is so strong on the palate. If you think about it, the two strongest impressions you have with meat are texture and aroma. You bite down and it's a pleasing sensation as your teeth meet resistance from flesh. Then you breathe out and the mildy funky bouquet of the meat, which is the heart of its distinctive flavor, rises up into your nose, pulling with it all the flavors that you have cooked into the meat with other ingredients. Meat is a foundation on which you can build a great Gothic cathedral of a recipe.

Oceanic

Fishy would have been the best word here — but it doesn't have the most mouthwatering connotations. When we say something smells fishy we're not being entirely fair to fish. The clear implication is that it is not a desirable way to smell. While that's probably true for fish that's been left standing out for a while, freshly caught fish smells cool, clean and appetizing. The aroma often referred to as fishy is really the bouquet that fish picks up when it's exposed to the air for too long.

As with meat, there are three components to the taste of fish. First there is a bouquet that is usually more restricted and focused than the bouquet of meat. This probably explains why fish allies so well with herbs, aromatic spices, and clean and bright broths with their accent on vinted or tangy flavors. Next, there is a part of the tasting that happens in the mouth and the palate. With white-fleshed fishes, the taste on the tongue is subtle, as opposed to a stronger taste with fish that have more oil, such as salmon or bluefish. Then, as with meat, you bite down and breathe out. The texture is a pleasant experience and helps to punctuate tastes, separating one from another. The breathing out lifts the defining aromas into the nose.

This whole matrix of fish and flavor — aroma, palate, and texture — is a taste that we call Oceanic. We thought of breaking out shellfish and giving them their own taste category but, for simplicity, we felt their characteristics are not wildly different from the finny fish. One thing distinguishing shellfish is that it sometimes has a buttery component that is found in only a few finny fish, such as monkfish.

That still leaves the thorny problem of where to put freshwater fish. Since trout, salmon, and steelhead will all migrate down into the ocean when given a chance, they could register to vote in fresh or saltwater. Pike, the freshwater basses, blue gill, crappie, sturgeon, and so on are not oceangoing but they still share most of the characteristics of ocean fish without that light hint of iodine in their bouquet. So for now, the river and lake fish sit with their oceangoing brothers and sisters, milder in taste but recognizably the same class of food.

Starchy

Starchy foods have a dual personality. When boiled or baked they are soft and mushy. When fried, however, they are at the exact opposite end of the texture spectrum. In fact, there is nothing crispier than starch that is fried in some hot oil. This property is one of the important elements in our discussion of toppings in the second section of this book, "The Elements of Cuisine: The Chef's Larder," which consists of a number of subrecipes, many of them made in advance, that will allow you to assemble whole platoons of taste elements without having to spend all day in the kitchen.

Rice, potatoes, turnips, artichoke hearts, bread, barley, and quinoa all marry well with stronger flavors, diffusing and extending them. Although much is made of serving fish and vegetables at the peak of freshness, that is probably no more important than serving starch just after you've cooked it. It actually has a fresh flavor. The longer it stands before serving, the more it acquires the taste of a bite out of the telephone book.

As with meat and fish, the starch taste platform is only secondarily a mouth taste. The primary function is textural. Starch coats the tongue and calms down or diffuses more strident tastes. It cleans off the palate and gets you ready for the next fusillade of strong flavor. This is not to place a value judgment on strong vs. bland. You need both in order to effectively taste your way through a complex dish. If you've ever gone to a winery to do a barrel tasting of recent vintages, you'll have found that those first few tastes of wine are quite pronounced and delicious. As you sip, swirl, and shpritz through 20 or 30 wines, you could be served a Romanee Conti that fetches a thousand dollars a bottle and your tongue would respond with the energy of an overfed uncle snoozing in front of the television.

TASTES THAT PUNCTUATE

In the total experience of taste, we have talked about a three-part process: aroma, mouth taste, and texture. This last element serves to punctuate taste. Crunch is a signal to stop one taste experience and start another, kind of like a period or a colon in a sentence. Smoothness, which rounds out tastes, works like a comma, extending the experience of tasting.

Texture helps you to "read" longer taste messages and to make sense out of them. It separates or unites the layers in a recipe. It emphasizes some and mutes others. Think of vanilla ice cream with chocolate chips in it, or the crackly crust on fried chicken: these foods are in fact unthinkable without those texture elements that set off the different tastes. Texture, as we have seen, in meat, vegetables, poultry, and seafood, serves as important a role as taste on the palate. Fat and oil — which are major elements in cuisine — are not tastes per se. They are closer to texture, their chief function is to disseminate taste, spreading it on the palate and launching it, as aroma, into the nose. Fat in a recipe works like the commas that link a long elegant sentence.

Texture is a critical part of tasting, but it is not taste: it has no flavor. Speaking in those terms, there is only one true taste element that we use to punctuate, the one we are calling sharp bitter.

Sharp Bitter

When we mentioned the taste receptors on the tongue, we left one out: bitter. Watercress is bitter. Almonds have a bitter note to them, and so do spinach, cold beer, and Campari. Cranberries are fruity, but they are also bitter. Scientists tell us that recognizing bitter is a way for us to avoid poisonous foods or things that might harm us. But beer is bitter and so is red wine, and to date we have yet to come upon a sound reason for avoiding them.

Bitter usually serves to bring taste on the palate to a full stop. This is a good thing when strong tastes begin to cascade and over-whelm your senses. A taste may be enjoyable and, for some of us, even ecstatic, but if you have too much you become drunk on it and lose the ability to enjoy and understand the fullness of the recipe. For the sake of simplicity we will also include the notion of sharp in this taste category. Horseradish is bitter but it's something else too, and that something else is sharp. Sharpness feels a little bit like bitter with some picante heat in the bouquet. It stops taste on the tongue but also rein-forces the effect of aromas that pull flavor.

TASTE AS NARRATIVE

A recipe is more than a mere combination of ingredients and techniques. There is a fourth dimension to every recipe. It is put together over time and it is experienced over time. Like a story or a song, it has a beginning, middle, and end: it has a *narrative*. So, while we list the ingredients and detail the preparation, we don't end it there. That would be rather like looking at the sheet music and never hearing a performance. At the end of every one of our recipes we have tried to explain the taste experience from beginning to end, from first aroma to last lingering aftertaste. That's the reason that we spent so much time identifying and describing tastes.

Not everybody will experience every taste to the same degree that we did. You may have a lower threshold for detecting salt and a higher one for floral herbal aromas. Nevertheless, pretty much everyone will experience tastes in the sequence that we lay out. Those of you who are used to reading descriptions of wine will recognize the format.

We have found that thinking about recipes in this way has helped our understanding, not only of the recipes that we have made but also in thinking about new recipes and combinations. It has also deepened our appreciation of the work of other chefs (including the many home chefs we know who prepare food that stimulates the palate and the mind). By way of example, here is a simple recipe with its accompanying taste narrative:

OVEN-CRISPED CHICKEN WITH MAPLE VINEGAR SAUCE

THIS IS A FAST, easy way to make very crisp chicken and *everybody* in the history of humanity loves crispy chicken. Instead of serving it with biscuits and honey, which is traditional in the South, we made it with a maple vinegar sauce, which adds sweetness through maple syrup. We topped it with cranberries, almonds, and shallots, which have the bitterness to cut sweet richness and the nuttiness to work with the maple syrup. Serve with Wilted Endives, Cranberries, and Yams (page 126).

SERVES 4–6

SAUCE

2 tablespoons butter

¼ cup chopped shallots

½ teaspoon cracked black pepper

¼ teaspoon nutmeg

⅓ cup cider vinegar

⅓ cup maple syrup

———

Melt the butter in a medium saucepan over medium-high heat. Add the shallots and cook, stirring occasionally until they are soft and translucent. Add the pepper and nutmeg. Add the vinegar, bring to a boil, then add the maple syrup. Return the sauce to a boil and cook until it returns to maple syrup thickness. Set aside.

CHICKEN

1 3- to 4-pound chicken (have butcher splay the chicken open so it lies flat)

Kosher salt

Freshly ground white pepper

2 tablespoons grapeseed or other neutral vegetable oil

———

Preheat the oven to 500 degrees. Make an incision in each of the chicken's thighs, then tuck in the legs. Season the chicken on both sides with salt and pepper. Heat the oil in a large heavy ovenproof skillet over high heat. Place the chicken, skin side down, in the hot pan then immediately transfer it to the oven. After 10 minutes, flip the chicken. Continue roasting, basting every so often, until the thigh juices run clear, 25–30 minutes total roasting. Remove the chicken from the skillet and allow it to rest for 5 minutes. Pour the fat from the roasting pan and deglaze over medium low with the Maple Vinegar Sauce. Cook just until the sauce thickens, less than a minute, then set aside in a warm place.

TOPPING

¾ cup slivered almonds

3 tablespoons butter

½ cup dried cranberries

½ cup leeks, finely sliced then measured

1 tablespoon dried homemade bread crumbs

Kosher salt

Freshly ground white pepper

———

Combine the almonds and butter in a small skillet. Heat over medium-high heat and cook, turning the almonds frequently, until they are golden brown. Add the cranberries and leeks. Continue pan-roasting for 1 minute. Add the bread crumbs and season with salt and pepper.

PLATING

———

Cut the chicken in serving size parts. Arrange the chicken on warm plates. Spoon first sauce, then topping, over the chicken and serve.

OUR TASTE NOTES

First there is a tangy vinegar aroma and, right along with it, nuttiness from the almonds and butter. The crunchiness from the chicken skin and intense saltiness follows. There's a smooth overall sweetness from the maple syrup, cut by the bitter cranberry and the nuts. The cranberry also has tang, which works with the vinegar to pull out more meaty taste. The flesh of the chicken gives texture and punctuation, plus a full meaty aroma. The end notes are sweet, meaty, and salty.

In looking over this recipe you probably noticed that it is somewhat different in layout from the average Sunday newspaper recipe that usually has one list of ingredients followed by the steps in assembling the recipe. There is a reason for that. There are various parts to most of the dishes in this book — a sauce, a main ingredient, a topping, and so on. We have written them in a way that they will go together most easily. The maple vinegar sauce, above, should be prepared first, then the cranberry almond topping, then the chicken. If you do this, following each mini-recipe within the master recipe, the final dish will come together quickly and easily.

Success is all about prep, and we have tried to order the recipes so that the prep follows logically and most easily. It also allows you to clean up as you go in most cases. Do the maple vinegar sauce, rinse the utensils, then do the next part. In this way, you don't end up like Lucille Ball in the famous episode of *I Love Lucy* where she is constantly running to keep up with an assembly line at the chocolate factory. The long and the short of it is that even the most complicated recipes can be broken down into a series of simple recipes. The secret, according to the French, is "mise en place" or, according to the Boy Scouts' motto, "Be prepared!"

THE GOLDEN THREAD

Think of each recipe in this book as a short story. Think of all the courses in the meal as a novel that has a beginning, middle, and end. Quite often when someone shows us a menu for an upcoming meal, the individual dishes may be great but the meal as a whole makes no sense: it has no *taste logic*. Any well-planned menu is a progression of flavors reaching a crescendo with the main course and a final resolution in the dessert. To find the golden thread that truly unites a meal, you must pay attention to the transitions between dishes. A diva who begins a song on her highest note is like a chef who starts a meal with flavors that are too strong: there's nowhere to go. In planning a satisfying meal, that first impression is critical and so is the last. This is not to suggest that there is only one right way to plan a menu, but rather to encourage you to realize that for a chef, planning and preparation are the same as with any artist contemplating a performance.

For example, a summer supper might start on a bright note with Two-Tomato Coulis with Three Basils (page 130) to wake up your palate. Next, a grilled Snapper Filet with Crisp Capers, Apricots, and Shallots (page 161) has strong, defined tastes, yet they aren't heavy, and they build on the tang of the tomato starter. Then Oven-Crisped Chicken with Maple Vinegar Sauce that we just described, because it has the fun of Southern fried chicken and the sweetness of barbecue sauce without being fried and without being thick and cloying. Notice how the maple from the chicken picks up the sweet and tang from the apricots and capers in the second course and carries them into new combinations. Finally, for dessert an espresso Petit Pot (page 50), which is the lightest custard and also gives you the coffee palate that one likes at the end of a meal.

This book by no means seeks to exhaust the discussion of taste. Instead it very much seeks to start one, to get people thinking about taste as it is used in cooking and experienced in dining. To do that, we worked with the materials at hand: in this case the recipes and culinary point of view of one chef. These recipes are largely a portrait of one chef's work. We think the same method can be applied to any-one's cooking, and will result in a deeper understanding and better food. It is our hope that when you have finished this book, you will know more than a recipe or two (which is, face it, all we take from most cookbooks). Just like a professional chef, you should feel confi-dent that you can look in any pantry, any refrigerator and know how to take the ingredients at hand and combine them in a sure, confident, and delicious way. It's elemental.

Everyone has had the experience of eating something in a restaurant and saying, "Gee, I really wish I could make that at home." And for a moment, you fantasize that, starting from scratch, you will go home and whip up all the deep brown sauces that sent your tongue into sensory overload, or that pear tart with the creamy fruit-filled topping that nudged you off the diet wagon.

Nice fantasy, but it's probably not going to happen. You see, chefs rarely start dishes from scratch (although occasionally a last-minute inspiration strikes and is sent out into the dining room for its maiden tasting). More often, chefs assemble dishes as they are ordered, from elements that have been prepped in advance. If you go into any big-time restaurant kitchen at eight in the morning, there are caldrons of stock boiling away and huge roasting pans full of bones and caramelizing vegetables. As the morning progresses, the cooks and sous-chefs take many of these elements and strain, reduce, season, and balance them (while some may simmer or marinate for a day or two). By the time diners show up, all that remains from the tumult of those first frantic hours are a few little pots of sauce on the stove, some chopped vegetables in little bowls, some meat that has been marinated or braised, and maybe a few spice mixes in even smaller bowls. All this preparation is just waiting to be thrown together the minute the waiter calls for "Two oxtail risottos for table twelve, extra truffles!"

In the second section of this book, "The Elements of Cuisine: The Chef's Larder," we offer you a number of made-in-advance elements of cuisine that you can have on hand to create our recipes or to combine in your own creations. They can be your secret weapons in making more complex food or in whipping together a simple but fascinating combination of tastes and textures. Every great chef resorts to these kinds of elements to make food that is more interesting and individual. Few share them.

Many of these elements are discrete flavor packages, or "add-ons" to the featured ingredient in a recipe. Often, they provide concentrated high flavor in midtaste, or a beginning flavor that acts as an overture. They may also effect a transition from one taste to the next, just like a passing tone in music. Once you develop your innate ability to recognize and combine tastes — that is, once you become conversant in the language of taste — you'll begin to invent your own add-ons. That will mark a critical step in developing your own cooking style.

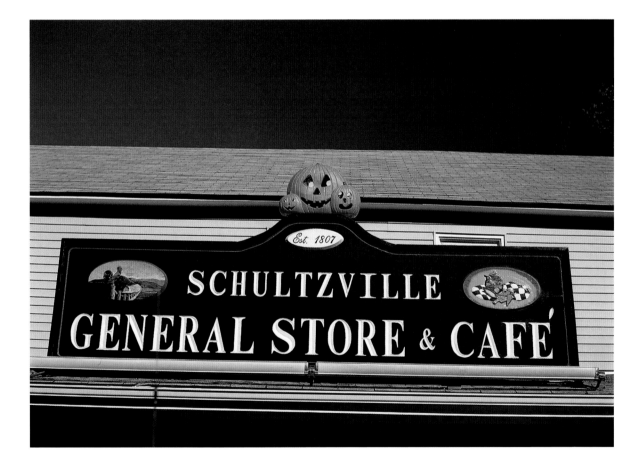

THE FOURTEEN ELEMENTS OF TASTE

TASTES THAT PUSH

Like a wave approaching shore or a wind blowing across the plains, these tastes push everything forward.

SALTY

PAN ROASTED SALMON WITH AROMATIC SALTED HERBS

WE WANTED TO SIMPLIFY
the long process of a traditional
gravlax, by making a fresh herb
and salt topping with gravlax
ingredients. The tastes would be
the same, but rather than infusing the salmon, the taste of the
topping remains distinct and lets
the nice texture of cooked salmon
come out while still preserving
the oomph of the spices and salt.

SERVES 4

HERBS

2 tablespoons thinly sliced chives
½ cup finely chopped parsley
⅓ cup finely chopped mint
⅓ cup finely chopped dill
_____

Combine the herbs in a large bowl.

SALT AND SPICE MIX

1½ tablespoons coarse salt
⅛ teaspoon cayenne pepper
⅛ teaspoon ground cardamom
½ teaspoon ground nutmeg
½ teaspoon coarse ground white pepper
_____

In a separate bowl, combine the salt and spices.

SALMON

2 tablespoons peanut or other neutral vegetable oil
4 6-ounce salmon fillets, each about 1 to 1½ inches thick, skin on
Kosher salt
Finely ground white pepper
Cayenne pepper
2 tablespoons butter
_____

Preheat the oven to 225 degrees. Heat the oil in a large ovenproof
skillet over medium-low heat. Add the salmon, skin side down, and
cook until crispy, about 2 minutes. Season to taste with salt, pepper,
and cayenne. Dot the salmon with butter and place it in the oven
for about 4 minutes. (The salmon will look rare in the middle and
more fully cooked on the outside.) Remove from pan. Arrange the
fillets on warm plates then sprinkle with herbs. Dust lightly with salt
and spice mix and serve.

The first taste note is salty. It pushes everything else forward. Next you bite through the spice mix and floral herbs until you meet the tooth resistance of the fish. All of the flavors mix at this point. The aromatic herbs help focus the big flavor of the salmon. The parsley softens the spices. The bulby chives pull up more flavor. The mint works with the nutmeg to pull sweetness out of the salmon. As generations of gravlax makers have known, dill's freshness marries well with salmon. The end notes are oceanic from the salmon, salty, and piquant from the pepper.

PORK TENDERLOIN WITH BOURBON
MUSTARD BRINE AND TANGY PEARS

OUR FIRST TRY with this recipe was good but incomplete. All that salt and the sharpness from the whiskey fairly cried, "Give me something tangy and sweet to cut the strong briny pork!" There just happened to be a few ripe pears in the fruit bowl. We cut them in slices, as you would for a tarte tatin, and cooked them quickly in some white vinegar and refined sugar. It was just what was called for.

SERVES 4–6

PEARS

2 tablespoons distilled white vinegar

1 tablespoon sugar

2 soft ripe pears, peeled, quartered, cored, and then sliced into crescents about ¼ inch thick

———

Combine the vinegar and sugar in a saucepan. Add the pears. Bring to a simmer and cook, stirring occasionally, until the pears are barely tender, 2–3 minutes. Taste—the pears should be both tangy and sweet—and add a pinch of sugar if necessary. Set the pears aside in a warm place.

PORK

1½ pounds boneless pork tenderloin

2 cups Bourbon Mustard Brine (page 234)

2 tablespoons grapeseed or other neutral vegetable oil

———

Cut the pork into medallions approximately ¾ inch thick. Marinate the pork in the Bourbon Mustard Brine in refrigerator overnight.

———

Heat the oil in a cast-iron skillet over medium heat. Pan-roast the pork, turning once or twice, until it is well browned on all sides, about 7–10 minutes. (Be careful: the honey in the brine can burn quickly so you must keep turning the meat.)

PLATING

———

Put two medallions on each warm plate. Place the pears so that a few slices sit on the pork and a few alongside it on the plate.

OUR TASTE NOTES

As you bite through the pork, the tang and fruit of the pears pulls out all the meatiness and salt. The mustard and the bitterness in the bourbon help cut these overpowering tastes so that you start the whole process over again with your next bite of pear. The last notes are sweet, tang, salt, and a long lingering meatiness.

GLAZED SCALLOPS AND CAPER, ALMOND, SHALLOT TOPPING

SCALLOPS ARE AN EX-
TRAORDINARY carrier of flavor
considering they are just a simple
white piece of flesh. They are
light enough for a ceviche yet
probably their most surprising
characteristic is they have a slight
funkiness in them, unusual in
seafood. This allows us to cook
them with shallots, and with
truffles. It also allows us to serve
them with really strong earthy
wine like a Haut-Brion, usually
reserved for heavier meats and
game. The bay scallops that are
available in the fall are the perfect
ingredient in this dish.

To accent the deep fresh
flavors in the scallops, we went to
our larder and chose a Madeira
Mirin Glaze. The saltiness and
sweetness in it pretty much cried
out for a topping, so we went
back into our larder, scratched
our collective chin, and went with
a version of our caper, almond,
shallot mix that we had played
around with in a few dishes.

SERVES 4 AS A FIRST COURSE

GLAZE

½ cup warmed Madeira Mirin Glaze (page 196)

TOPPING

3 tablespoons butter
½ cup sliced (raw) almonds
4 tablespoons small brined capers
2 shallots, finely diced
Kosher salt
Freshly ground white pepper
1 tablespoon chopped parsley

_____

Melt 1 tablespoon of butter in a skillet over medium-high heat. Add the almonds and toast, stirring frequently until fragrant and golden, about 1½ minutes. Transfer the almonds to a plate and wipe out the skillet.

_____

Add another tablespoon of butter to the pan and heat over medium-high heat. Add the capers and crisp. Return the almonds to the pan and add the shallots. When they begin to color, swirl in the remaining butter. Season with salt and pepper and add the parsley.

SCALLOPS

½–⅔ pound bay scallops, rinsed and patted dry
2 tablespoons corn or other vegetable oil
½ tablespoon butter (optional)
Kosher salt
Freshly ground white pepper

_____

Heat the oil in a heavy skillet over high heat. Get it good and hot. Add the scallops and sauté — the flesh is delicate, so resist the temptation to move them around — until they are golden on one side, about 1 minute. Flip them over and cook about 30 seconds more. (You may, optionally, finish them off with butter.) Season with salt and pepper.

PLATING

Spoon the glaze onto four plates. Divide the scallops among the plates. Spoon the topping over the scallops and serve.

OUR TASTE NOTES

First you get the salt of the soy from the glaze. Then there is the vinegary tang and sweetness from the Madeira and rice wine vinegar in the glaze. You get crunch from the almonds and a contrasting softness from the scallop. The different textures are a big part of this dish. The almonds, which are bitter, close down the salt and tang of the capers. The final note is floral herbal from parsley; the last echo is ginger.

BRINED VENISON WITH JUNIPER BLACK PEPPER BURGUNDY SAUCE

IN THE FALL, wildlife is foraging on berries, nuts, and apples, which are all ripe, fully developed foods. Game meat in this season is rich and flavorful and can stand up to a powerful sauce. In this recipe you finely dice your caramelized vegetables because they will stay in the finished sauce (in many other dishes you discard those caramelized vegetables after the recipe is cooked). The sauce supports the game flavors but also cuts them so that each mouthful starts the flavor process again. Serve this sauce with stronger game, like woodcock, grouse, venison, or elk. Don't confine it to game, though. It's lovely with pot roast or a roast filet mignon. We liked this with pinot noir in the sauce, because it has the strength that game seems to want. A nice malbec would work equally well.

SERVES 4

VENISON AND BRINE

4 venison chops, about 1 inch thick
2 cups Juniper Game Brine (page 232)

———

Marinate the venison in the Juniper Game Brine overnight.

SAUCE

1 cup Basic Red Wine Sauce — Venison Variation (page 221)

FINISHING

2 tablespoons grapeseed or other neutral vegetable oil
Brined venison

———

Heat the oil over medium-high heat. Add the venison and sauté for about 3 minutes on each side for medium rare.

PLATING

———

Spoon the sauce onto four plates, place a venison chop on each, and garnish with the reserved caramelized vegetables.

OUR TASTE NOTES

A strong vinted aroma opens the bouquet. Next, the crunch and sweetness of the caramelized vegetables. The salt pushes the meat flavor. Butter rounds out the sharp edges of the wine, and juniper bouquet pulls up all the flavors. Next comes the texture and funkiness of the meat. The last tastes are a mix of wine, butter, pepper, and the sweet nuttiness of the roasted vegetables. They coat the palate and smooth the overall taste.

PICANTE

SWEET SCALLOPS IN A PINK LENTIL CRUST WITH A HOT-AND-SWEET BELL PEPPER REDUCTION

THIS DISH SURROUNDS THE PALATE with the gentle and hot sides of pepper. The sweet bell peppers give a garden and tangy foundation to the strength of the cayenne. The cayenne pushes with its picante heat. The lentils rather than being a mushy side dish, are there for crunchy punctuation. The sauce would go well with veal, grilled fish, a gutsy ratatouille or any dish with zucchini or summer squash.

SERVES 4 AS A FIRST COURSE

SAUCE

¼ cup extra virgin olive oil

½ medium onion, sliced

2 cloves garlic, thinly sliced

1 tablespoon thyme leaves, chopped

½ cup roughly chopped red bell peppers

Kosher salt

Freshly ground white pepper

Cayenne pepper

Pinch sugar

2 cups chicken stock or water

1 tablespoon butter

⅓ cup celery leaves, roughly chopped

———

NOTE: It is one of the crimes of many supermarkets that they trim the celery leaves off the stalk before they put it out in the cooler. We find celery leaf to be a fresh, lively herb and we use it often.

———

Warm the oil in a saucepan over medium-high heat and toss in the onion, garlic, and thyme. Mix to coat with oil, then add the peppers. Season with a little salt, pepper, cayenne, and sugar (you start seasoning now because you will render out water quickly), then add stock or water. Bring to a simmer, then cover and reduce the heat to low. Cook gently until the peppers are very tender, about 10 minutes.

———

Puree the pepper mixture and strain through a fine sieve. Return the puree to the stove and reduce until thick enough to coat the back of a spoon (or watch the bubbles — when they start to make slow blurps, you're getting there). Swirl in the butter and bring to a froth with an immersion blender (or by whisking vigorously). Correct the seasoning with salt, cayenne, pepper, and sugar and keep the sauce warm over very low heat.

SCALLOPS

1 pound bay scallops

About ½ cup Pink Lentil, Turmeric, and Green Peppercorn breading
(page 190)

2 tablespoons grapeseed or other neutral vegetable oil

1 tablespoon butter

———

Pat the scallops dry. Coat one side of each scallop with the
breading.

———

Heat a skillet over medium-high heat. Add the oil then the scallops,
coated side down. Let them cook, undisturbed, until the breading crisps,
about 1 minute. Flip and finish cooking for about 30 seconds more.

PLATING

———

Spoon the sauce into four shallow bowls. Place scallops in the
middle, and garnish with celery leaves.

OUR TASTE NOTES

This is a very complex taste. It comes through first as crunch, then
salt, and then heat. Next you get sweetness from the scallops. The
pepper sauce brings garden brightness and major heat at the finish.
The celery leaves provide a final garden note with some bitterness
to close down the taste.

STRIPED BASS WITH CARAMELIZED SCALLIONS
IN GREEN PEPPERCORN CITRUS SAUCE

THE LAST TEN YEARS has witnessed the return of the striped bass to the waters of the Northeast. In addition to being a great game fish, it is a great cooking fish. It has delicate-tasting white flesh, but is firm enough to grill or barbecue. It doesn't have too many bones; it is easy to cut; and it has a cooked texture that helps it pull out big flavor from sauces and toppings without disappearing into the background.

SERVES 4

SCALLIONS

18 thin scallions
2 tablespoons extra virgin olive oil
Kosher salt
Freshly ground white pepper
2 tablespoons butter

———

Trim 16 of the scallions to about 5 inches. Blanch the 2 remaining scallions until the green tops are flexible. Cut the tops into two long strips and use these strips to tie the trimmed scallions into bundles of four. (If this sounds complicated, all you are doing is making some bundles without string.)

———

Preheat the oven to 350 degrees. On top of the stove, heat a large ovenproof skillet over low heat. Film the skillet with oil then add the scallions. Season with salt and pepper and pan-roast, turning the scallions occasionally until they are nicely browned, about 5 minutes, then transfer to the oven and continue cooking 15 minutes, then add butter and cook until the scallions are tender, about 5 minutes more.

SAUCE

1 cup warmed Tangy Green Peppercorn Sauce (page 225)

FISH

2 tablespoons extra virgin olive oil
4 6-ounce striped bass fillets, skin on
Kosher salt
Freshly ground white pepper
Zest of 1 lemon, julienned

———

Heat a large skillet over medium heat. Film the skillet with oil. Season the fillets on both sides with salt and pepper and sauté until golden (and just warm in the center), approximately 3 minutes per side for a 1-inch-thick fillet.

PLATING

Spoon the sauce on four warmed plates. Place a fillet, skin side up, on each plate. Prop the scallions against the bass, then garnish with lemon zest and serve.

OUR TASTE NOTES

The clear clean taste of the sauce rides above everything tangy and salty. The bulbiness of the scallion pulls up the sweetness and the roundness of the oil, honey, and butter: a big bouquet. The tarragon pulls up sweetness as well as the oceanic taste of the striper. The fish has toothy texture that calms the strident tastes in the sauce. The final notes are tanginess and heat, and echoing sweetness.

RICE FLAKE CRUSTED SALMON WITH CHILE CITRUS SAUCE

CITRUS IS AN EFFECTIVE WAY to achieve strong concentrated flavor without fat. Ginger is one of those ingredients that serves as a bridge between flavor elements. It has floral notes, fruitiness, and mild heat. In addition to its own spiced aromatic character, it can help ally disparate flavors such as chili and lemongrass, honey and basil. This sauce can be used with flounder, halibut, or striped bass.

SERVES 4

SAUCE

2½ cups fresh-squeezed orange juice, strained

⅓ cup mirin (sweet rice wine available in Asian markets)

1 stalk lemongrass, sliced and very finely chopped

2 tablespoons peeled chopped fresh ginger

1 dried hot chili

Kosher salt

1 tablespoon sugar

_____

Combine the orange juice, mirin, lemongrass, ginger, and chili in a saucepan. Simmer over medium heat until the mixture has reduced to the consistency of a light syrup. Season with salt and sugar. Discard the chili and keep the sauce warm over low heat.

SALMON

1 egg plus 1 yolk, whisked together

4 teaspoons flour

Kosher salt

Freshly ground black pepper

4 6-ounce salmon fillets, 1–1½ inches thick, skin on

1 cup Crispy Rice Flake Crust (page 191)

2 tablespoons extra virgin olive oil

1 tablespoon butter

_____

Combine the egg and flour. Whisk until smooth then whisk in ½ teaspoon salt and ¼ teaspoon pepper.

_____

Brush the skin side of each fillet with egg and flour binding. Press this coated side of the salmon into the seasoned rice flakes.

_____

Heat a large skillet over medium-low heat, add the oil, then the salmon, crust side down. Sauté the fillets until the crusts are golden brown, 3–4 minutes, then add the butter and turn the fillets. Cook 2 minutes longer for medium-rare. Season to taste with salt and pepper.

PLATING

Spoon the sauce onto four warmed plates. Place a salmon fillet on each.

OUR TASTE NOTES

There is a very strong crunch at the outset. Then the oceanic flavor of the salmon comes out as you bite through the fish. The sweet tanginess of the sauce comes forward next. Then the fruitiness of the orange accented by the fruity floral side of the ginger. The ginger and chili pod pack powerful picante heat. This extends the oceanic salmon taste at the finish.

SWEET

BIGGER EGG NOG

CONSIDERING ITS RICH TASTE, egg nog often seems a bit insubstantial and overly liquid. By heating the yolks ever so gently and then combining them when chilled with the egg whites, the result is an egg nog whose warm sweetness can stand up to the chilliest New Year's Eve. Surprisingly, this egg nog wasn't invented in the cold of the northern winter. For that matter it wasn't even invented for New Year's Eve at all, but rather for Boxing Day at the Peninsula Hotel in Hong Kong.

SERVES 4

INGREDIENTS

¾ cup heavy cream

6 eggs, separated

½ cup plus 2 teaspoons sugar

1 cup cognac

½ teaspoon ground star anise

1 teaspoon ground cinnamon

¼ teaspoon ground allspice

½ teaspoon ground nutmeg

1 cup milk

——

Beat the cream until it forms stiff peaks, then refrigerate.

——

In a double boiler set over simmering water, combine the egg yolks, ½ cup sugar, and cognac. Whisking constantly, cook the egg mixture until it thickens slightly, is warm to the touch, and looks satiny and white (a zabaglione-like consistency), about 5 minutes. Stop the mixture from overcooking by whisking it over ice, then refrigerate.

——

Combine the remaining 2 teaspoons sugar, spices, and egg whites in a medium bowl or mixer and whisk to stiff peaks. Chill over ice.

——

Fold the chilled egg white mixture gently into the chilled egg yolks, then, again very gently, fold in the chilled whipped cream, adding the milk a little at a time as you go. Refrigerate until ready to serve.

SERVING

——

Serve in chilled glasses or egg nog cups, with a pinch of allspice.

OUR TASTE NOTES

The aromatic spices hit your nose first, pulling up sharp grape aroma from the brandy. All at once you get the sweet, round, satiny taste of the cream and eggs with spiced aromatic highlights from the nutmeg and allspice, pulling at the sweetness.

WATERMELON AND TOMATO SALAD

AS THE FRUITS AND VEG-
ETABLES of summer ripen, developing their sugars, there's no
reason to confine sweetness all by
itself to the dessert course. This
salad combines succulent watermelon and tomatoes at their peak;
they give a dominant note of
sweetness to a recipe that carries
tangy and floral overtones. It goes
perfectly with soft shell crabs, fried
fish, barbecued chicken or ribs.
The taste combination is one that
is as bright as the seashore on a
clear July afternoon. So take a hint
from the season, and serve these
with grilled fish, and India Pale Ale
cold enough to break a heat wave.

SERVES 4

WATERMELON REDUCTION

1½ cups chopped seeded watermelon

1½ tablespoons honey

1 tablespoon fresh lemon juice

Chinese chili oil, to taste

Kosher salt

Freshly ground white pepper

———

Puree and then strain the watermelon. Transfer the strained liquid to a
saucepan and simmer over medium heat until reduced by two-thirds.
Add the honey, lemon juice, and chili oil and mix well. If using immediately chill in a stainless-steel bowl, over ice. Otherwise chill in the refrigerator for at least 2 hours. Adjust the seasoning with salt, pepper, and
additional chili oil if desired and refrigerate until ready to serve.

SALAD

2 medium firm ripe tomatoes, seeded and diced (about 1 cup)

2 cups diced watermelon, seeded

1 tablespoon celery leaves

1 tablespoon chopped fresh thyme leaves

⅓ cup finely diced celery root

1 tablespoon extra virgin olive oil

Kosher salt

Freshly ground white pepper

FINISHING

———

Just before serving, combine the tomato, watermelon, celery leaves,
thyme, celery root, and olive oil in a bowl. Add the watermelon
reduction, toss gently, then season with salt and pepper.

PLATING

———

Mound the salad on chilled plates using a few bits of diced celery root
and celery leaves as garnish, then serve immediately. (This is important
because the tomato and watermelon will begin to get watery once the
salt is added.)

Honey and watermelon highlight the sugars in all of the ingredients. The crunchiness of the watermelon (if it isn't crunchy you have let the salad sit too long before serving) is reinforced by the celery root. The celery leaves and herbs, as well as the honey, have a slightly floral edge that pull out the other flavors. The tang of the lemon juice focuses and continues to pull these same flavors. The chili oil strikes a picante chord that strengthens the fruity and fresh garden tastes of the salad.

IN THE SPRING, many people have the impression that every taste is delicate and retiring, but that's not really the case. Ramps (wild spring onions) couldn't be sharper, and popcorn sprouts (baby corn shoots) are highly sharp and sweet. Similarly, rhubarb, which is the centerpiece of this dish, is the most puckeringly tangy food you can think of. Here we use ice cream and some aromatic spices to make this rambunctious early spring fruit (or is it a vegetable?) behave very nicely in a dessert.

SERVES 4–6

INGREDIENTS

1¾ pounds fresh rhubarb, trimmed and roughly chopped (about 8 cups)

6 cups water

1 cup sugar

1 vanilla bean, split

1 cinnamon stick

1 teaspoon ground nutmeg

⅓ cup fresh lemon juice

———

Combine the rhubarb, water, sugar, vanilla bean, cinnamon, and nutmeg in a saucepan and bring to a boil. Reduce the heat to medium and simmer until the rhubarb is very tender (almost falling apart), about 20 minutes. Strain the mixture through a cheesecloth then chill over ice, if using immediately. Scrape the black seeds of the vanilla bean into the soup. Otherwise chill in refrigerator. Season with lemon juice and additional sugar if necessary and refrigerate until ready to serve.

GARNISH

2 stalks rhubarb, peeled and thinly sliced (about 1 cup)

2 tablespoons sugar

½ cup water

———

Combine the sliced rhubarb, water, and sugar in a saucepan and simmer gently over medium about 3 minutes, no longer. Set aside and allow to cool.

ICE CREAM

4 small scoops vanilla ice cream

3 tablespoons toasted pignoli nuts

———

Scoop the ice cream into four balls then roll the scoops in the pignoli nuts.

PLATING

Place the ice cream scoops in four chilled bowls. Ladle soup around the ice cream, garnish with rhubarb slices, and serve.

OUR TASTE NOTES

A strong spiced aromatic bouquet at the start, as the nutmeg and cinnamon pull up sweetness. The smoothing effect of the sweetness is further rounded by the vanilla. The pignolis' nutty flavor adds roundness. Their crunch punctuates between the tart soup and the sweet smooth ice cream. Tanginess from the rhubarb and lemon soup is the strong underlying flavor. It is reinforced by the crunchy rhubarb slices. The roundness of the ice cream mellows the long-lasting tang of the rhubarb. Both tastes fade slowly.

CHILLED LEMONGRASS SOUP

THIS STARTED FROM THE
IDEA that milk could pick up
the volatile oils in lemongrass and
diffuse them. From that notion,
it was a quick jump to thinking
about the floral and fruity side of
lemongrass in a delicate dessert
(rather than as an enhancement to
more savory dishes). The trick with
this soup is for everything, including the bowls, to be cold. Try some
other garnishes such as diced
pineapple or shaved coconut.

SERVES 4

INGREDIENTS

4 cups milk
2 vanilla beans, split lengthwise
2 cups chopped lemongrass
6–7 tablespoons sugar

———

Combine the milk, vanilla, lemongrass, and 4 tablespoons of the
sugar in a saucepan. Bring to a low simmer over medium heat.
Remove the pan from the heat, cover and let cool to room temperature. Strain, squeeze seeds from the vanilla beans into the liquid,
and chill over ice or for at least 2 hours. When well chilled, adjust
the sweetness with the remaining sugar. Refrigerate until ready to
serve.

GARNISH

½ papaya, peeled, seeded and cut first into long wedges then into
    thin triangles

ICE CREAM

4 small scoops coconut-pineapple, burnt almond, or vanilla ice
    cream
⅓ cup chopped almonds, toasted

———

Scoop the ice cream into four balls then roll the scoops in almonds.
Reserve any remaining almonds for garnish.

PLATING

———

Divide the papaya among four chilled soup bowls. Place a scoop of
ice cream in the center of each bowl, then surround with lemongrass milk. Garnish with almonds and serve immediately.

OUR TASTE NOTES

The floral side of the lemongrass and the vanilla intensifies sweetness. The roundness of the ice cream is mildly diffused by the milk.
The crunch from the almonds punctuates between the soup and
ice cream. The papaya, a faintly funky fruit, cuts the sweetness.

CHOCOLATE TRUFFLE

IN NORTHERN EUROPE, elder-flower syrup—bright, floral, and sweet—is often used in place of sugar or honey. It also has a tang that cuts through sugar. Strong chocolate with a syrupy fruity tang is an unbeatable dessert combination. It also can be overwhelming. By combining it with fruits and berries, grilled pineapple slices, caramelized bananas, or diced mango you get a powerful finisher to a meal without being bludgeoned with sweet richness.

MAKES ABOUT 2 DOZEN

INGREDIENTS

½ cup heavy cream

1 egg, separated

9 ounces bitter chocolate, chopped

3 tablespoons butter, room temperature

3 tablespoons elderflower concentrate

⅓ cup golden raisins soaked in brandy and chopped

4 tablespoons slivered almonds

_____

Whip the cream to stiff peaks, then refrigerate.

_____

Whisk the egg white to stiff peaks. Refrigerate.

_____

Combine the chocolate and butter in a bowl. Melt the mixture, by placing the bowl over hot water and stirring. Add the elderfower syrup (or liqueur) and egg yolk, mix well, then stir in the raisins and almonds.

_____

Fold in the whipped cream and beaten egg white. Chill thoroughly.

_____

SUBSTITUTION NOTE: We love elderflower syrup, which is available in many delicatessens that stock Swiss, German, or Scandinavian ingredients. If you can't find it, you can substitute raspberry, apricot, or other fruit syrups or your favorite liqueur but you will have to experiment with the quantities a little because sugar content may vary.

FINISHING

_____

Form the chocolate into balls about the size of large marbles and serve.

OUR TASTE NOTES

Sweet creamy roundness and the burned light bitterness of chocolate begin the taste. The raisins bring on fruitiness. The elderflower follows and cuts through with its sweet tang. Roundness, sweetness, and fruity bouquet linger at the end.

WARM RASPBERRIES AND ELDERFLOWER CURD

CHARLES SCHULZ, who created the "Peanuts" comic strip, is partly responsible for this dessert as well as a number of others in this book. You see, when Chris Broberg, the Lespinasse pastry chef, was five years old, he had a Scottish nanny who brought him lemon curd. "Why can't we have this every morning?" asked Chris (who even then had developed the sweet tooth that would dominate his life). His parents heard the conversation and bought him a "Peanuts" cook-book that had a recipe for lemon curd. Chris made it, and to this day he says that experience is what made him become a chef. Thank you, Charles.

SERVES 4

CUSTARD

3 whole eggs
2 yolks
13 ounces elderflower concentrate (see substitution note on page 54)
½ cup sugar
⅔ cup butter

———

Combine all of the ingredients in a medium saucepan. Whisking constantly, cook the mixture over medium-low heat until it thickens enough so the spoon leaves a trail as you mix (the consistency of a thick béchamel), about 7 minutes.

———

Press the elderflower curd through a fine strainer and chill over ice.

RASPBERRIES AND NUTS

1½ cups raspberries
3 tablespoons sugar
2 tablespoons raspberry liqueur (framboise)
¼ cup orange juice
Juice of ½ lemon
2 tablespoons heavy cream
1 tablespoon chopped pistachio nuts

———

Combine the raspberries, sugar, liqueur, and orange juice in a medium saucepan and heat over low heat until the raspberries are well warmed but not yet cooked. Season with lemon juice and set aside. Reserve the cream and nuts for garnish.

PLATING

———

Place a large spoonful of the elderflower curd in the middle of four chilled plates. Spoon warm raspberries over the curd, drizzle cream around the outside of each plate, garnish with pistachios, and serve.

OUR TASTE NOTES

The elderflower curd fills the mouth and nose with floral, creamy sweetness, before pushing forward the sweetness of the raspberries. The framboise and citrus reinforces this and the alcohol cuts it.

TASTES THAT PULL

Where the "push" tastes have a tendency to put their shoulder into it and push all taste forward, the "pull" tastes seek out underlying flavors and highlight them.

TANGY

TAMARIND IS USED in Asian and Indian cooking for its fruity tangy properties. It is as common as lemon or vinegar in Western cuisine. Tang in barbecue sauces and fresh salsas cuts the heaviness of meat.

SERVES 4

SALSA

2 tablespoons grapeseed or other neutral vegetable oil

½ red bell pepper, seeded and diced

Kosher salt

Freshly ground white pepper

Cayenne pepper

1 tablespoon sugar

½ cup diced jicama

1 mango, peeled, pitted, and roughly diced

1 tablespoon white vinegar

———

Heat the oil in a large skillet over high heat. Add the bell peppers and sauté, stirring occasionally, until they begin to brown slightly. Season with salt, pepper, cayenne, and a pinch of sugar. Add the jicama and cook, stirring occasionally, until just warm but still crisp, then add the mango and remove from the heat. Season with vinegar and remaining sugar.

GLAZE

About ½ cup warmed Tamarind Barbecue Glaze (page 195)

FLANK STEAK

1½ pounds flank steak

2 tablespoons grapeseed or other neutral vegetable oil

Kosher salt

Freshly ground black pepper

Cayenne pepper

½ cup roughly chopped cilantro (reserve for garnish)

———

Brush the steak with oil, season with salt, pepper, and cayenne, and grill (over hot coals if possible) about 3–4 minutes on each side for medium-rare.

PLATING

———

Slice the steak on the bias, coat with tamarind glaze, garnish with the salsa and chopped cilantro, and serve.

After the initial crunch, teeth meet meat. The floral herbal coriander pulls up the garden vegetables. The bell pepper comes forward, fruity then sweet and tangy. The mango pushes forward fruit and sweetness and then passes off to the fruity tamarind tang. Throughout, the texture and meatiness of steak counterbalance the fruit and defuse it.

BARBECUED SEA TROUT WITH
GRAPEFRUIT–GINGER–SHALLOT SAUCE

GRAPEFRUIT IS AN INTERESTING ingredient because it is one of the few that combines both bitter and sweet (milk chocolate is another). Bitter closes down the palate, which helps to confine the taste of highly flavored foods so that you can begin each bite with a clean slate, so to speak. Everything else in this recipe pushes and pulls flavor. There is hardly a taste that this combination doesn't push forward or pull up. It works beautifully to pull out the flavor in more subtly flavored and delicate ingredients such as fresh white-fleshed fish, baby shrimp, or bay scallops.

SERVES 4

SAUCE

1 cup fresh grapefruit juice
1 tablespoon finely diced shallots
1 teaspoon finely chopped ginger
2 tablespoons sugar
Kosher salt
Cayenne pepper
Pinch paprika
Juice of ½ lemon
1 grapefruit, peeled, pith removed, segmented, then cut into wedges
2 tablespoons julienned grapefruit zest

_____

Combine the grapefruit juice, shallots, ginger, sugar, salt, cayenne, and paprika and bring to a simmer over medium-high heat. Allow the mixture to reduce by half, then adjust the seasoning with salt, lemon, sugar, and cayenne (the sauce can be made up to an hour in advance up to this point).

_____

Just before serving, add the grapefruit sections to the warm sauce. (Reserve the zest for garnish.)

FISH

2 tablespoons grapeseed or other neutral vegetable oil
4 6-ounce sea trout fillets, skin on (you can also use any firm white-fleshed fish)
Kosher salt
Freshly ground white pepper

_____

Brush the fish lightly with oil, season with salt and pepper, then grill (over hot coals if possible), 2–3 minutes per side.

PLATING

_____

Spoon the sauce onto four warm plates. Place a fillet in the center of each plate, then garnish with grapefruit zest and serve.

The tang, bitterness, and sweetness of the grapefruit are pulled further by the tang of the lemon. Then comes the floral herbal of the ginger joined by the bulbiness of the shallot. The sugar pushes the sweet fruit, while the lemon and grapefruit tang pulls out flavor. The texture of the sea trout punctuates and its ocean flavor diffuses the attack of the sauce. In this mix of powerful and concentrated flavors, the fish is the final note, with trailing echoes of bitter, sweet, and, finally, cayenne heat.

THE GREAT ANGLING and food writer, A. J. Maclane, observed that after working with fresh seafood, your hands smell like cucumber. Here we play on the watery garden crunch of cucumber as counterpoint to the pearly smoothness of tapioca and the ocean taste of the crab. Tapioca, by the way, can give body and light texture to savory dishes and does not always have to be thought of as a school cafeteria dessert. Serve cold — the colder the better — which means that you will need to be bold with the seasoning.

SERVES 4

SOUP

½ cup plain whole milk yogurt

1 cup unsweetened coconut milk

2 tablespoons pearl tapioca, medium size

1 cup water

3 seedless cucumbers, peeled and chunked

2 cups roughly chopped honeydew melon

½ cup heavy cream

Kosher salt

Sugar

Juice of 1 lemon

1 teaspoon whole coriander seeds, measured then ground

1 teaspoon whole cumin seeds, measured then ground

1 tablespoon grated ginger

Freshly ground white pepper

———

Drain the yogurt for several hours or overnight in a strainer lined with cheesecloth set over a bowl.

———

Combine the coconut milk, tapioca, and water in a medium saucepan and heat over a low flame until the mixture is well thickened and the tapioca pearls are soft and translucent, about 20 minutes. Set aside to cool.

———

Puree the cucumber and honeydew, then strain through a fine sieve.

———

Chill the puree in a bowl set over ice. Whisk in the cream and drained yogurt. Season with salt and sugar, then whisk in the tapioca (just enough to thicken up the sauce — don't feel that you have to use it all). Mix in the lemon juice, coriander, cumin, and ginger, then season to taste with salt, sugar, and pepper. Refrigerate until ready to serve.

CRABMEAT

2 tablespoons extra virgin olive oil

1 cup cooked crabmeat

Juice of 1 lemon

¼ cup chopped parsley

Kosher salt

Freshly ground white pepper

———

Combine the olive oil, crab, lemon juice, and parsley in a bowl and season well.

GARNISH

¼ cup finely diced cucumber (a mandoline helps here. First cut
   the cucumber in long strips on mandoline then finely dice)

¼ cup julienned carrots

½ teaspoon fresh thyme leaves

½ teaspoon chopped lemon zest

1 tablespoon chopped mint

PLATING

———

Use a small ring mold or round cookie cutter to neatly mound the seasoned crab in the center of four chilled soup plates. Ladle soup around the crab. Garnish each serving with cucumber, carrots, thyme, lemon zest, and mint and serve.

OUR TASTE NOTES

The sweet fruitiness in the soup is first pulled up by the floral herbal mint. Then the coconut nuttiness joins the yogurt's creaminess and the crab's buttery roundness. This is accented in texture by the smooth, slithery tapioca. The floral herbal tang in the citrus zests and lemon juice sharpens the fruit and vegetables. The crunch in the cucumber garnish leads back to sweet and garden tastes; they are also pulled up by the aromatic spices, which persist as a final note along with light picante heat.

THIS IS A PRIME EXAMPLE of what we call a "Chef's Dessert." Most desserts start with the idea of something sweet and just keep building on sweetness. Thus, soufflés — which can be wonderful and light — often are just a mound of overpowering sweetness. Here, the idea that started the dessert was tanginess and then using only enough sugar to balance it. The trial and error that went on between chef and pastry chef required Chris Broberg, the pastry chef at Lespinasse, to run up the three stories to the chef's office about a hundred times before the dessert was just right. But pastry chefs can always use a little extra exercise to stay trim.

SERVES 6

FRUIT

3 tangerines

3 lemons

3 passion fruits

Approximately 2 cups sugar (don't worry, you bake the filled fruit on top of mounds of sugar, you don't include this all in the recipe)

———

Preheat the oven to 475 degrees. Slice about ½ inch from the top of the tangerine, then cut the lemon, lime, and passion fruit in half. Scoop out the flesh of each fruit, taking care not to rip the citrus rinds (you have an extra just in case). Set the rinds aside. Press the fruit through the sieve, then sweeten the juice to taste (the juice should still be sour but have some sweetness to it). Passion fruit requires no sweetening.

———

Divide the sugar between six forms of a cupcake tin (each cup should be about one quarter full). Place a reserved rind in each sugar-filled cup. Spoon a tablespoon of citrus juice into each and set aside.

SOUFFLÉ BATTER

4 egg whites

2 egg yolks

4 tablespoons granulated sugar

1 tablespoon powdered sugar

———

Put the egg whites and yolks in separate bowls. Put half the sugar in each bowl. Whisk the yolks until they thicken and have a satiny sheen. Whisk or beat the egg whites until they are firm enough to pull up into peaks but not so stiff that they stand up and remain that way. Fold half the egg whites gently into the yolks. When they are fully combined, fold in the rest. Spoon the soufflé batter into the fruit rinds. Place the soufflés in the lower third of the oven and bake until they rise and brown, 6–7 minutes. Dust with powdered sugar. Serve immediately.

The fluffiness of the soufflé is matched by the sugary sweet aroma of the first bite. The very tangy and lightly sweet fruit juice in the bottom of the rind comes as a surprise. The floral note in the fruit juice further pulls up the round and creamy sweetness of the soufflé.

VINTED

LOBSTER IN SYRAH REDUCTION WITH AROMATIC GRITS

GOING BY THE old red-wine-with-meat and white-wine-with-fish rule, lobster is forever thought of as being prepared with white wine. But lobster has a rich, buttery-tasting flesh that can stand up to a big red wine sauce. You can use whatever red wine you like, but we liked a syrah because it is favored in the Rhône, and the Rhône flows to the sea where lobsters are caught and brought upriver to Lyon, which is the capital of modern gastronomy (roundabout logic but it made sense to us). Generally lobsters are way overcooked. This is a soft way of cooking them beautifully that preserves the silky texture of the meat.

SERVES 4

SAUCE

1 cup warm Basic Red Wine Sauce —lobster variation (page 221)

GRITS

1 cup milk
½ cup water
Kosher salt
Freshly ground white pepper
Pinch ground nutmeg
2½ tablespoons quick-cooking grits
2 tablespoons butter

_____

Combine the milk, water, and a pinch each of salt, pepper, and nutmeg in a saucepan and bring to boil. Add the grits, and simmer until soft (1–2 minutes). Finish with 2 tablespoons of butter. Season again and adjust thickness with more milk if necessary.

TOPPING

2 tablespoons medium diced leeks
1 tablespoon butter
Kosher salt
Freshly ground pepper

_____

Lightly sauté leeks in butter. Season.

LOBSTER

4 whole lobsters, 1–1½ pounds each
3 tablespoons butter (or olive oil)
Kosher salt
Freshly ground white pepper

_____

Preheat the oven to 350 degrees. Blanch the lobsters for 3 minutes in boiling water. Remove and shock in ice water. Separate tails and

split lengthwise. Remove the meat and discard the vein that runs the length of the tail. Remove meat from claws. (Put empty shells, heads, and bodies in zip-lock bag and freeze for future lobster stock.)

———

Place the lobster meat in a well-buttered baking dish.

———

Dot the lobster with butter. Season with salt and pepper or cayenne and place in the oven, 5–6 minutes.

———

NOTE: This will yield a lobster that is still a bit translucent. If you like your lobster cooked till it is white all the way through, leave it in the oven a few more minutes.

PLATING

———

Place a dollop of grits in the middle of four wide bowls. Ladle the wine sauce and vegetables around the grits. Place the lobster on the grits and spoon butter from the lobster dish over lobster. Top with the sautéed leeks.

OUR TASTE NOTES

If, like most people, you go straight for the lobster and grits, you'll find that you get the round nose of butter that pulls up the shell-fish flavor, itself a bit buttery. The grits spread taste and coat the palate. The rich lobster flavor and texture is cut by the vinted tang of the wine. The slight bitterness of the wine-infused vegetables tends to contain taste. The leeks fill the nose and pull up the next round of taste. The final notes are butter and wine with a little picante heat.

TURKEY LEG IN CHIANTI TOPPED WITH PAN-ROASTED WINTER VEGETABLES

THE TUESDAY BEFORE

THANKSGIVING, our plans to catch (and prepare) striped bass were undone by a cloud bank that rolled in over Montauk. We went to Dreeson's Market in East Hampton where we were obliged with two turkey legs. This is one of the results: the Turkey Leg Provençale is the other (page 110). Tarragon is an unusual garnish for turkey, but notice how its affinity for sweetness pulls up flavor from the carrot, onions, wine, and dark turkey flesh. This is a perfect recipe for an empty nest Thanksgiving, or, come to think of it, while you are still courting and there are no extra mouths to feed . . . yet.

SERVES 4

INGREDIENTS

2 turkey legs (drumstick and thigh) from a 12-pound turkey
Kosher salt
Freshly ground white pepper
3 tablespoons corn or other neutral vegetable oil
6 slices bacon
4 carrots, roughly diced
1½ cups diced celery root
1 cup diced onion
1 leek, white part only, sliced
2 whole heads of garlic
2 bottles Chianti or other medium-bodied dry red wine
2 bay leaves
10 white peppercorns
4 cloves
6 sprigs thyme
1 sprig rosemary
1–2 tablespoons sugar
½ cup tarragon, roughly chopped (measured then chopped)
4 tablespoons butter

_____

Preheat the oven to 325 degrees. Score the turkey legs with incisions approximately ¼ inch deep (this allows deep and even cooking). Season the legs liberally with salt and pepper. Heat the oil in a large ovenproof skillet over medium-high heat and sear the turkey on all sides. (Don't be shy on the searing. This means more than just browning on the very outside. Get it good and caramelized.) Remove the turkey from the pan and toss in the bacon. Cook until the fat starts to render, about 30 seconds. Add the carrots, celery root, onion, leek, and garlic. When the vegetables are well caramelized, remove half of them to a small bowl and set aside. Return the turkey legs to the pan. Add the wine, bay leaves, peppercorns, cloves, thyme, rosemary, and 1 tablespoon of sugar, and bring to boil.

Cover the pan and braise in the oven, until the turkey is tender, about 2½ hours. Set aside (up to this point the recipe may be done ahead of time).

TO FINISH

_____

Remove turkey from pan and set aside. Degrease the braising liquid, then heat the vegetables in the liquid over medium-high heat. Allow the liquid to reduce until it is the consistency of thin maple syrup, then add the butter and swirl. Adjust the seasoning with salt, pepper, and sugar. Lower the heat to medium (so that the thickening liquid is bubbling vigorously but not sticking and burning). Place the turkey back in the pan. Baste the turkey with the sauce as you cook (this will give you an impressive glaze). Continue basting until all the sauce is used up in the glaze.

_____

Meanwhile in a separate skillet, pan-roast the reserved vegetables over medium-high heat until tender and warm, about 3–4 minutes. Add the tarragon and scatter this topping over the turkey.

_____

For a rustic touch — and for less dishwashing — serve the turkey in its cooking pan.

OUR TASTE NOTES

Redolent of turkey flesh, this is a smooth sauce with a wine tang that pulls flavor. The licorice note of the tarragon pulls up the fruit in the wine. As you bite down and exhale, the meat texture holds your taste attention. The pepper bouquet rises in waves, as does the bulbiness of the onion. Caramelized vegetables add sweetness and celery root adds starchiness. The end notes combine the big wine tang, the tarragon's floral herbal focus, picante heat, and, underpinning it all, the roundness of butter and strong meat flavors.

PAN-SEARED SCALLOPS IN A WHITE WINE BROTH WITH BUTTERNUT SQUASH

WE TRIED THIS RECIPE with Gardiner's bay scallops that our friend Sam Lester had harvested. The scallops were so good they almost brought the inevitable question "Why bother with recipes when you can sauté them in butter or eat them raw with lemon juice and herbs?" You can. On the other hand, scallops flattered with the attentions of Chardonnay and honey and the briskness of lemon juice are pretty nice, too.

SERVES 4 AS AN APPETIZER

BROTH

1 tablespoon butter
¼ cup finely diced shallots
½ cup finely diced butternut squash
1 cup Chardonnay (or Riesling)
2 tablespoons honey
3–4 teaspoons lemon juice
Kosher salt
Freshly ground white pepper
Cayenne pepper

_____

Melt the butter in a medium saucepan over medium-high heat. Add the shallots and cook, stirring occasionally, until they are soft. Add the squash, wine, honey, and lemon juice. Season with salt, pepper, and cayenne and bring to a boil. Adjust the seasoning with salt, pepper, and lemon juice and keep warm over very low heat.

SCALLOPS

2 tablespoons grapeseed or other neutral vegetable oil
1 pound bay scallops
2 tablespoons butter
1 tablespoon lemon juice
Kosher salt
Freshly ground white pepper

_____

Heat the oil in a large pan over medium-high heat. Pat the scallops dry and sauté — don't shake or move the pan — until they are golden on one side. Don't season them either. (If you were to salt them at this point, you would extract a lot of water and dry them out.) When the scallops are caramelized, approximately 2 minutes, shake them slightly to roll them in the pan. Add butter, lemon juice, and finally, seasoning. Baste with the browning butter very briefly (15 seconds, just to coat the scallops evenly). Drain the scallops for a second on paper towels.

PLATING

Divide the scallops among four bowls. Ladle broth into each bowl and serve.

OUR TASTE NOTES

The floral note of honey sounds first. The vinted element from the wine pulls flavor forward as does the lemon tang. The squash gives crunch and roundness, which brings out the roundness in the scallop. A light heat and salt, with faint oceanic tones and sweetness, finish off the taste.

STEAMED SOLE IN ROSE CHAMPAGNE EMULSION
WITH FAVA BEANS AND SPRING PEAS

THE CHARDONNAY GRAPE from which champagne is made works well with seafood. There is a long-term affinity between champagne and sole. We chose rose instead of white wine for the aesthetics of the look. Favas and spring peas are light early season vegetables. With the pink champagne and the white-fleshed fish, lightness is the theme here.

SERVES 4

SAUCE

2 tablespoons finely diced shallots

1½ cups pink champagne

3 tablespoons butter

Kosher salt

Freshly ground white pepper

Cayenne pepper

Pinch sugar

Lemon juice (to taste)

¼ cup chive lengths (about ½ inch)

———

Combine the shallots and champagne in a medium saucepan and bring to a boil. Reduce by three-quarters, then lower the heat to a simmer and whisk in butter. Season with salt, pepper, cayenne, and sugar. Balance with lemon juice. Just before serving beat with an emulsion blender (or whisk vigorously), then add the chives and serve warm.

VEGETABLE

1 cup peeled fresh fava beans (remove outer shell, blanch, drain, then remove the skin; the beans pop out easily)

1 cup shucked peas, blanched, and shocked in ice water (you may substitute other seasonal vegetables such as baby spinach or new leeks)

1½ tablespoons butter

Kosher salt

———

Melt the butter over medium-low heat in a small saucepan. Add the fava beans and peas. Season with salt and gently warm.

FISH

1½ pounds skinless sole fillet, divided into 4 portions

2 tablespoons butter

2½ tablespoons finely diced shallots

Cut the fillets lengthwise in half. Roll them into little turbans, securing the fish with a toothpick, and place in a steamer. Dot the fish with butter and sprinkle with shallots. Set the steamer over boiling water and steam until the fish is translucent, 4–6 minutes. This will vary with the thickness of the fillet. Basically the fish is cooked when it first starts to flake.

GARNISH

2 tablespoons butter or olive oil

¼ cup medium diced tomato

1 teaspoon sliced chives

2 tablespoons diced celery leaves

———

Heat the butter or oil in a small skillet over medium-high heat. Add the tomatoes and half the chives and cook for 2 minutes.

PLATING

———

Place sole in bottom of four wide soup plates. Place the peas and fava beans on the turbans and top with the tomato garnish, the remaining chives, and the celery leaves. Ladle the champagne sauce around the fish.

OUR TASTE NOTES

Leek and shallot bulbiness precedes the vinted tang of the champagne, which is reinforced by the lemon juice. The sugar pushes and balances the tang. The fish is mostly texture, with a light oceanic taste. The favas and peas both have garden notes and crunch. Favas, being a little starchy, calm down the palate between acid and sweet tastes. The celery leaves — lightly bitter — in the topping do the same, while the tomatoes push tang and sweetness. The last notes are bulby and vinted, lengthened by the roundness of butter.

CHILLED STRAWBERRY SOUP AND CHAMPAGNE ICE

WITH SO MUCH CONCERN about fat in the diet, many chefs have compensated for low fat by raising the intensity of flavor. This makes for a bedeviling problem in creating a smooth transition from final entree to dessert. The meat, fish, or fowl course is often laden with powerhouse flavor. So is the dessert, but it is flavor of a different kind. The extreme sweetness and creaminess of most desserts will fight a meaty or fish entree. When you are going to bridge between two complex sets of flavors, that bridge needs to strive for depth as well as effective transitional tastes and textures.

SERVES 4

SOUP

NOTE: All the ingredients should be cold before you start.
3 cups strawberries, hulls removed
⅓ cup champagne
⅓ cup sugar
½ cup fresh orange juice
Juice of 1 lemon

———

In a blender, pulse strawberries, champagne, half the sugar, and half the orange juice (the mixture should be slightly chunky). Chill. When the soup has chilled down, adjust consistency and taste with the remaining sugar, orange juice, and lemon (strawberries vary greatly in consistency, sweetness, and tang). Refrigerate.

CHAMPAGNE ICE

3 cups champagne
6 tablespoons sugar
Juice of 1 lemon
⅓ cup honey

———

Combine ingredients and freeze in a flat tray until it has the consistency of sorbet. Shave by running a tablespoon along the sorbet, which will come away from the flat tray in curls.

GARNISH

3–4 strawberries, sliced (you will need 3 slices per serving)
Zest of 1 lime, julienned

PLATING

———

Pour the soup into four chilled soup plates. Place a scoop of champagne ice in the center of each. Garnish with strawberry slices and lime zest, and drizzle with champagne. (We like to serve this with a light crisp cookie.)

The floral bouquet of the lime zest hits the palate first. The champagne, working with citrus juices, brightens the fruitiness. The strawberry slices add texture and echo the stronger fruit tastes in the soup. Likewise, the scoop of sherbet echoes the champagne and sugar in the soup, and its smoothness creates the impression of creaminess. The cookie gives snap and a buttery sweetness that prolongs the overall flavor.

BULBY

CONFIT OF VEAL BREAST WITH BULBY VEGETABLES

ON A VISIT TO WAINSCOTT, Long Island, in the late fall, a bright warm Sunday turned into a cool foggy Monday by the shore. We started out with the idea of something light, which brought us to the idea of using the juices of bulby vegetables. As the ocean damp seeped into our bones, we began to crave more richness. So we kept reducing liquid as we cooked our way through this recipe, and the result was a meaty bulby dish with layers of sweet warming richness and a delicious glaze. The directions look lengthy but this is a quick and simple rustic dish. It is also quite beautiful and dramatic to present at the table.

SERVES 4

INGREDIENTS

3 pounds veal breast

Kosher salt

Freshly ground white pepper

½ cup corn or other neutral oil

2 large shallots, peeled

1 medium onion, quartered

1 leek, split and washed

12 cloves garlic, unpeeled

⅓ cup diced celery root

2 bay leaves

4 cloves

1 tablespoon white peppercorns

½ teaspoon whole cumin

½ cabbage, cored and quartered

2 cups dry white wine

1⅓ cups apple cider

⅓ cup chive lengths (about 1 inch long)

———

Preheat the oven to 250 degrees. Season the veal liberally with salt and pepper. Heat the oil in a large ovenproof skillet or Dutch oven over medium-high heat. Add the veal and cook, turning to brown on all sides. When the veal is nicely browned, transfer it to a plate. Add the shallots, onion, leek, garlic, celery root, bay leaves, cloves, peppercorns, and cumin to the pan and cook, stirring occasionally, until the onions begin to brown. Toss in the cabbage and cook it until it wilts and browns slightly, then add 1 cup each wine and cider. Season with salt, cover, and braise in the oven until the meat is falling-off-the-bone tender, about 2½ to 3 hours (this will vary with the thickness of the veal breast). Remove the cooked veal and vegetables from the liquid and keep warm. Strain the braising liquid through a fine sieve.

———

Degrease the braising liquid and return it to the pan. Add the remaining wine and cider, bring to a boil, and reduce to the consistency of maple syrup. Adjust the seasoning with salt and pepper, return the meat (but not yet the vegetables) to the pan and simmer, basting with the braising liquid until the sauce is almost syrupy and the meat nicely glazed.

———

Just before serving, place the reserved vegetables around the veal and caramelize the glaze in a preheated broiler. Garnish with chives and serve.

OUR TASTE NOTES

This is a many-layered yet smooth-tasting dish. The white pepper hits the nose first, followed by wave after wave of bulby vegetables. The cabbage blends in with the bulby vegetables lending a note of sweet funkiness. Its aroma focuses the other tastes. The veal is first experienced as intense meaty bouquet. As you bite into it, its texture comes forward and highlights the apple sweetness, vinted wine tang, and again the sugary, bulby bouquet of cooked onions and leeks.

HALIBUT WITH SPRING ONION STEW IN WATERCRESS-MUSSEL BROTH

LOOKING OVER THE INGREDIENT LIST in this recipe, you are most likely to notice the halibut, mussels, and pink lentils, before the onions. But this is definitely a dish built on onions. Onions aren't glamorous, but the bulbiness of onions is one of the only ways to pull out the sweet and delicate taste of seafood without overpowering it.

SERVES 4

WATERCRESS BROTH

2 bunches watercress

1 tablespoon butter

2 tablespoons finely diced spring onions (or scallions)

1 clove garlic, slivered

⅓ cup roughly chopped fresh ginger

2 cups chicken stock

1 cup water

———

Pluck 1¼ cups of watercress leaves and reserve for topping. Melt the butter in a saucepan over medium-high heat. Add the onions, garlic, and ginger and cook, stirring occasionally, until fragrant. Add the remaining watercress (stems and all) to the skillet. Add stock and water, cover, and simmer about ½ hour. Strain the broth through a fine sieve and reserve 1 cup for the stew and the remaining liquid for the sauce.

SPRING ONION STEW

2 tablespoons butter

1 bunch spring onions (or three medium white onions), thinly sliced

Kosher salt

Freshly ground white pepper

1 cup watercress broth (see above)

———

Preheat the oven to 300 degrees. Melt 1 tablespoon butter in a large ovenproof skillet over medium-high heat. Add the onions, season liberally with salt and pepper, and cook until the onions have softened. Add the cup of watercress broth, and bring to a simmer. Cover the pot and braise in the oven until the onions are very tender, 30–45 minutes. When the onions are so soft they are creamy, remove the skillet from the oven. Add the remaining butter and brown, stirring constantly, over medium-high heat. Set the onions aside in a warm place.

MUSSELS AND SAUCE

1 tablespoon butter

2 tablespoons finely diced spring onions (or scallions)

2 dozen mussels

1 cup white wine

Kosher salt

Freshly ground white pepper

1½–2 cups watercress broth (see above)

———

Melt the butter in a large pot over medium-high heat. Add the onions and cook until soft and translucent. Add the mussels and wine and season with salt and pepper. Cover the pot, increase the heat to high, and cook until the mussels open, usually less than 5 minutes (this depends on the thickness of the pot and how much heat your stove throws off). Drain the mussels, reserving the cooking liquid. Remove mussels from shells and set aside. Discard the ones that haven't opened.

———

Strain the mussel cooking liquid through a fine sieve and place it in a saucepan. Add the watercress broth, season with salt and pepper, and heat over medium-high heat until hot. Beat with an emulsion blender (or whisk) until frothy.

HALIBUT

4 6-ounce skinless halibut fillets

Kosher salt

Freshly ground white pepper

2 tablespoons grapeseed or other neutral oil

———

Season the halibut liberally with salt and pepper. Heat the oil in a large skillet over medium-high heat. Add the halibut (skinned side up) and cook until browned and flaky, 2–3 minutes per side.

TOPPING

4 tablespoons pink lentils

1 tablespoon corn oil

2 tablespoons finely diced onions

Kosher salt

Freshly ground white pepper

4 breakfast (or other small) radishes, finely sliced

½ cup scallion or green onion tops, sliced

1 cup reserved watercress leaves (see above)

1 tablespoon butter

———

In a spice grinder or mortar, grind the lentils medium fine. Heat the oil in a medium skillet over medium heat. Add the lentils and pan-roast until fragrant. Add the onions, season liberally with salt and pepper, and continue cooking, stirring occasionally, until the onions brown. Remove the pan from the heat and toss in the radishes, scallions, and watercress. Throw in the butter and toss until it melts. Adjust the seasoning.

PLATING

———

Place a spoonful of onion stew in the middle of four wide soup plates. Arrange the mussels around the stew and the halibut fillets on top. Garnish with the topping and additional reserved watercress leaves, then ladle the warm sauce over the mussels and serve.

OUR TASTE NOTES

There is salt in every part of this dish, sweetness from the onions and mussels, and sharpness from the radishes and watercress. The sharpness separates tastes and the sweet bulbiness of the onions pulls the flavor forward. The very first thing you go for is texture, and you get a double dose of that from the fish and topping. The salty onion crunch pulls out delicate fish flavor. The creamy onions and mussels are really two aspects of a soft round texture that embraces and enhances the sweet buttery shellfish.

GREEN ONION FONDUE

ALTHOUGH IT OFTEN makes the most sense to classify the taste of a dish by the way the final recipe hits the nose and palate, some recipes start from an ingredient and build on it. In the end, that ingredient may not be the overriding taste, but it is the starting point, the thing on which you build a recipe, taste by taste and texture by texture. In this case we started with mint and asked ourselves, "What goes with mint?" Since we were standing in front of the nut display, we didn't have to look far. There in front of us were pignoli nuts. We immediately associated them with North African cooking, which led us to dates. But as we added ingredients, we kept coming back to bulby onion notes to help round, smooth, and sweeten. So we started floral and ended up bulby. Serve with roasts or fish.

SERVES 4 AS A SIDE DISH

ONIONS

1 dozen medium scallions, trimmed
2 tablespoons extra virgin olive oil
Kosher salt
Freshly ground white pepper
1 teaspoon ajowan — an Indian spice related to caraway and cumin (you may substitute black onion seeds or cumin seeds)

———

Preheat the oven to 450 degrees. Cut the scallion bulbs into quarters lengthwise, leaving about two inches of green. Film an ovenproof skillet with the oil, add the scallions, season with salt and pepper, and place in the oven. Immediately reduce heat to 350 degrees. When the scallions start to blacken around the edges of the stem, about 4 minutes, turn them in the oil and cover the pan. Continue cooking until the scallions are nice and tender, 8–10 minutes more. Remove the pan from the oven, and sprinkle the scallions with ajowan seeds. Re-cover and set aside.

TOPPING

2 tablespoons butter
½ cup pignoli nuts
½ cup dried dates, chopped
Zest of 1 lemon, julienned
½ cup quartered cornichons
2 plum tomatoes, chopped
2 lemons, sectioned (squeeze and reserve juice from the remaining pulpy core)
Kosher salt
Freshly ground white pepper
1 cup mint leaves, cut in julienne

———

Melt the butter in a medium skillet over medium heat. Add the pignolis and pan-roast until they are fragrant and golden, 30 seconds or so, then add the chopped dates. When the dates soften,

about 1 minute, add the lemon zest and cornichons. Cook for another minute then toss in the tomato and lemon sections and juice. Season with salt and pepper and remove from the heat. Just before serving, add the mint.

SAUCE

1 pound plum tomatoes, pureed and strained
2 tablespoons extra virgin olive oil
Kosher salt
Freshly ground white pepper
Pinch sugar

————

Combine the strained tomato juice and olive oil in a large saucepan or high-sided skillet. Season with salt, pepper, and a dash of sugar and heat over medium heat, whisking, until the mixture steams but does not boil. Just before serving, beat with an emulsion blender (or whisk) until frothy.

PLATING

————

Divide the roasted scallions among four wide bowls. Ladle the tomato sauce around the scallions and garnish with the date topping.

OUR TASTE NOTES

The onion pulls up all of the tastes in this dish. The tomato and lemon combine for a tangy, fruity taste. Salt and tang (from the cornichons and lemon) come on as you bite down. The tomato liquid brightens everything. The softness of the onions helps to diffuse the strong topping tastes. The crunch of the nuts helps to punctuate. The sweetness of the onions is picked up by the dates and rounds out the sharp edges of the tang and salt. The last notes are tang and picante heat.

TENDER LEEKS AND TRUFFLES WITH POTATOES AND VINAIGRETTE

WHEN WE FIRST MADE THIS, young Jimmy Kunz, like a true ten-year-old son of a four-star chef, said, "Aw gee, Dad, truffles again!" Truffles may be a bit extravagant (actually there is no maybe about it) but we rescued ourselves from spendthriftness by making sure we used the potato skins.

SERVES 4 AS AN APPETIZER

INGREDIENTS

1 medium leek
12 baby leeks (or 6 medium leeks), peeled, trimmed, and washed
8 cups water
Kosher salt

—————

Peel away and discard the tough outer leaves of the medium leek then cut the tender inner leaves into ½-inch-thick ribbons the length of the leek. First blanch the leek ribbons, then the baby leeks in boiling salted water until tender, shocking each in ice water as soon as they are done. Reserve the blanching water. Drain and dry the leek ribbons. Drain and dry the baby leeks and cut into 2-inch lengths. Divide the baby leeks into bundles containing three leek lengths each. Tie each bundle with a leek ribbon.

TOPPING

1 cup corn or other neutral vegetable oil
3 Yukon Gold potatoes, scrubbed and peeled, peelings reserved and
   potatoes finely diced and reserved (see below)
Kosher salt
2 tablespoons sliced chives

—————

Heat the oil in a saucepan over medium-high heat. Deep-fry the potato peelings until they are browned and crisp, then drain on paper towels and season with salt. Reserve the chives.

POTATO AND TRUFFLE VINAIGRETTE

1 tablespoon butter
1 shallot, finely diced
2½ tablespoons chopped black truffles
3 Yukon Gold potatoes, finely diced (see above)
1½ cups reserved leek stock (see above)
2 hardboiled eggs, chopped
2 tablespoons chopped cornichons
1 teaspoon hazelnut oil

1 tablespoon grapeseed oil

2–3 tablespoons red wine vinegar

Kosher salt

Freshly ground white pepper

———

Melt the butter in a large skillet over medium-high heat. Add the shallot and sweat until soft and translucent. Add the truffles, then the diced potatoes. Stir to coat with butter, then add 1 cup of the leek stock. Simmer until the potatoes are tender, about 5 minutes, then remove from the heat and allow the potato mixture to cool to room temperature. Gently fold in the eggs, cornichons, hazelnut and grapeseed oils. Add vinegar, season liberally with salt and pepper, then set aside.

FINISHING THE LEEKS

2 tablespoons grapeseed or other neutral oil

Leek bundles (see above)

Kosher salt

Freshly ground white pepper

———

Heat the oil in a large skillet over medium-high heat. Add the leek bundles, season with salt and pepper, and brown on all sides.

PLATING

———

Spoon the potato truffle mixture into four wide bowls. Place leek bundles on top, garnish with crisped potato peelings and the reserved chopped chives, and serve.

OUR TASTE NOTES

A sweet bulbiness in the nose hits first, pulling up the tang of the cornichons and the salt. The funkiness of the truffles and eggs continues to expand the bouquet. The potatoes provide texture, coat the palate, and calm down the strong tang. The eggs, at this point, give an overall roundness to the mouth feel. Tang, picante heat, and truffle bouquet finish the taste.

TOMATO SUMMER ROLL WITH ONION HONEY MARMALADE

FOR THE START OF A SUM-
MER MEAL, this recipe draws
on the tang and bulbiness of our
onion marmalade to heighten the
fresh garden flavor of tomatoes at
their peak. To our way of thinking,
it's a case of taking something
perfect and making it even more
perfect. Pick the biggest, ripest,
gnarliest tomatoes you can.
Serve this right away, because the
salt in the marmalade and the
seasoning will pull water out of
the tomatoes.

Feel free to use this as an excuse
to buy a mandoline-type slicer to
slice the tomatoes nice and thin.
You will find that for slicing and
julienne cutting it is a wonderful
tool. Just be careful with your
fingers!

SERVES 4 AS AN APPETIZER

TOMATOES

5 beefsteak tomatoes, very thinly sliced, tops reserved
¼ cup Italian parsley, measured then roughly chopped
½ cup basil, measured then roughly sliced
1 tablespoon fresh thyme leaves
1 cup Onion Marmalade (see page 241)
3 tablespoons extra virgin olive oil

––––––

For each roll, lay out 2 rows of 3 overlapping slices of tomatoes on a small piece of plastic wrap. Combine the parsley, basil, and thyme and spread a little evenly over the tomatoes. Spoon onion marmalade on top of the herbs, then use the plastic wrap to lift and fold each tomato trio into a "burrito." Gently seal the plastic (the tomato slices will stick to one another like a flap on an envelope) and chill thoroughly.

GARNISH

2 tablespoons oil
Tomato tops (see above)
Kosher salt
Freshly ground white pepper
Pinch sugar
Drizzle extra virgin olive oil
⅓ cup chives, cut in ½-inch lengths
½ cup celery, finely diced
½ cup celery leaves
1 tablespoon thyme leaves
⅓ cup flat parsley leaves
⅓ cup basil, roughly slivered

––––––

Puree the tomato tops and pass through a fine sieve. Chill the puree, then season with salt, pepper, and sugar. (Trick: Put herbs and celery leaves in ice water. This will crisp them beautifully.)

PLATING

Put a circle of tomato coulis on the bottom of four chilled plates and drizzle with olive oil. Slip the plastic wrap off the tomato rolls and gently place a roll on each plate. Top with the chives, celery, and herbs and serve.

OUR TASTE NOTES

The vinted tang and bulbiness of the onions pull forward the honey's floral sweetness followed by the full fruitiness and garden notes of the tomato. The celery adds crunch and light bitterness to focus the big flavors in the onion marmalade. The herbs work as floral herbal, pulling up garden taste from the tomatoes and focusing the marmalade. They also add leafy crunch. Vinted tang, sweetness, and picante heat finish it off.

SPICED
AROMATIC

SPICED SHRIMP IN CARDAMOM ANCHO CHILI SAUCE

SHELLFISH STOCK is a good base for many recipes. It has buttery roundness and an oceanic but not "fishy" taste. Combining that basic French stock with Asian spices and Mexican chilies adds lots of flavor and complexity, which means you can make this sauce with less fat than a traditional butter-rich crustacean sauce. You could use this sauce with grilled or breaded white-flesh fish, poached oysters, and seafood risotto.

SERVES 4

SAUCE

2–3 tablespoons extra virgin olive oil

½ Spanish onion, chopped

4 cloves garlic, sliced

1 stalk lemongrass, roughly chopped

½ cup chopped celery root

1 cup sliced, peeled ginger

½ cup chopped coriander leaves

1 tablespoon coriander seed

1 ancho chile, seeded and roughly chopped

1 teaspoon kosher salt

1½ pounds medium shrimp, heads and shells removed and reserved (or, much better, have the fish store clean the shrimp and save the trimmings)

2 plum tomatoes, quartered

¾ cup coconut milk

2 tablespoons butter

―――

Film a large skillet with olive oil and heat over medium-high heat. Add the onion, garlic, and lemongrass and sauté, stirring occasionally, until they begin to brown. Add the celery root, ginger, fresh coriander leaves, coriander seed, and chile and sauté, stirring occasionally, 2–3 minutes (add more oil if the vegetables are sticking).

―――

Add the shrimp heads and shells and sauté 3 minutes.

―――

Add the tomatoes cook about 1 minute more, then add the coconut milk and enough water to cover. Simmer the mixture for 15 minutes, blend, then strain through a fine sieve. Return the sauce to the pan.

―――

Add the butter and froth with an immersion blender (or whisk vigorously). Keep warm over very low heat.

SHRIMP

Shelled shrimp (see above), deveined

3 tablespoons Ancho Cardamom Spice Mix (page 201)

2 tablespoons corn or other neutral vegetable oil

1 red bell pepper, seeded and diced

Kosher salt

Freshly ground white pepper

½ cup coriander leaves measured then finely chopped

½ cup flat parsley measured then finely chopped

———

Coat the shrimp with the spice mix, reserving any excess. Film a skillet with the oil and heat over high heat. Add the shrimp and sauté. As soon as shrimp start to turn pink, add the pepper. Continue to sauté for 3–4 minutes. Toss in the remaining spice mix. Remove the pan from the heat and add the sauce. Add the coriander and parsley and serve.

OUR TASTE NOTES

The first whiff is the sweet round creaminess of the coconut milk. This pushes the oceanic taste of the shrimp and the floral herbal lemongrass. The developing tastes combine subtly and well with the coriander. Peppers add crunch and their garden freshness punctuates the dish so that the ingredients of the sauce and spice mix are not constant and overpowering. The shrimp, too, provides texture and cleans up the palate from the strong sauce and spice mix. The shrimp isn't neutral, though: it has a buttery oceanic hue. Light heat and creamy sweetness from the initial taste return in the final notes.

FUSION IS A WORD we avoid because it is used so much that we are not sure what it means anymore. On the other hand, what you have here is kind of a bouillabaisse with sauce americaine and Oriental spices. If that is not fusion then, as the old rhythm-and-blues song says, "Grits ain't groceries, eggs ain't poultries, and Mona Lisa was a man!"

SERVES 4

AIOLI

½ cup Floral Herbal Aioli (page 223)

CROUTONS

1 thin baguette
About 3 tablespoons extra virgin olive oil
1 clove garlic, cut in half

———

Preheat the broiler. Thinly slice the bread, drizzle with olive oil, toast in the oven until golden, then rub with garlic.

MUSSELS AND BROTH

1 tablespoon extra virgin olive oil
1 tablespoon chopped shallots
1 tablespoon chopped ginger
1½ pounds mussels
Pinch saffron
2 cups water
2 cups white wine
2 tablespoons butter
¼ cup cognac
Kosher salt
Freshly ground white pepper
½ cup chopped curly parsley

———

Heat the oil in a pot over medium heat. Add the ginger and shallots and cook, stirring occasionally, until brown. Add the mussels and saffron. Add water and white wine. As soon as the mussels open, remove them from the broth and set aside. Discard those mussels that don't open. Add the cognac to the broth. Reduce by half and keep warm over very low heat. Take the mussels out of their shells. Discard the shells. Just before serving, add butter and beat the reserved lobster-mussel broth with an emulsion blender (or whisk) until frothy. Adjust the seasoning with salt and pepper and add the curly parsley.

FISH

1 teaspoon coriander seeds, toasted and ground

1 teaspoon cumin seeds, toasted and ground

½ teaspoon turmeric

1 teaspoon curry powder

1½ pounds monkfish, trimmed and cut into ½-inch cubes

Kosher salt

Freshly ground white pepper

2 tablespoons corn or other neutral vegetable oil

———

Combine the coriander seeds, cumin, turmeric, and curry powder. Roll the monkfish pieces in the spice mixture, then season with salt and pepper. Film a skillet with the oil and sauté over medium-high heat until the fish pieces are golden, 4 minutes total. You may toss the fish to cook evenly on all sides.

PLATING

———

Spoon the monkfish and mussels into four bowls. Ladle the broth around the seafood, then garnish each plate with a dollop of aioli. Serve accompanied by croutons and the remaining aioli.

OUR TASTE NOTES

You have every texture of seafood in this dish: soft mussels and toothy monkfish. The saffron, along with the curry and coriander, pulls strongly. A broader bouquet comes from the garlic. The aioli emulsion gives roundness. The fresh herbs add a crunch that punctuates the varied flavors and also build the complex bouquet. At the end there is aromatic spice in the nose and sweet oceanic notes on the palate.

THINK OF THIS as a Dixieland version of a classic ratatouille dish in which we substitute okra for eggplant. The real fun part of this recipe is the mung bean crêpe. We tried this one night and people kept asking for more of the crisp savory crêpes. The next night when we tested the Pork Tenderloin with Bourbon Mustard Brine and Tangy Pears (page 30) we had some crêpe batter sitting around and figured, what the heck? So we fried some up and used them as a savory note. Again people wanted seconds and thirds. Point of the lesson? Batter is better the next day. Second point? Crisp always wins. Third point, mung beans get very interesting when livened up with curry.

SERVES 4 AS AN APPETIZER

CRÊPES

½ tablespoon curry powder

1½ cups milk

¼ cup flour

Kosher salt

Pinch freshly ground white pepper

2 cups mung beans, soaked overnight in 3 cups water, drained

½ cup coriander leaves

½ cup cooked white rice

3 tablespoons extra virgin olive oil

———

Combine the curry powder, milk, flour, salt, pepper, and mung beans in a food processor and blend until smooth, 3–4 minutes. Refrigerate the batter until you have finished the ratatouille (below). Then, just before serving, film a large skillet with a little oil and heat over medium-high heat. Working in batches, spoon 2–3 tablespoons batter into the skillet, forming small pancakes. When the crêpes start to set, about 1 minute, top each with a sprinkling of coriander leaves and a thin layer of cooked rice. Let the crêpes set fully and flip. Crisp the second side and serve atop the ratatouille.

RATATOUILLE

1 cup split, seeded okra

2 large beefsteak tomatoes

8 red bell peppers, all seeded and 7 of them roughly diced

3 tablespoons grapeseed or other neutral vegetable oil

2 large onions, roughly diced

Kosher salt

Freshly ground white pepper

1 teaspoon ground cumin

Pinch each of saffron (about 12 threads), sugar, grated nutmeg, and cayenne pepper

Juice of 1 lemon

1 cup flat parsley leaves, measured, then roughly chopped

⅓ cup coriander leaves

2 tablespoons butter

_____

Blanch the okra in a large pot of boiling salted water then refresh in ice water and set aside. Puree and strain the tomatoes. Puree the remaining seeded bell pepper and reserve.

_____

Heat 2 tablespoons of the oil in a large skillet over medium-high heat and sauté the onions. When the onions turn translucent, add the chopped peppers. Season the mixture with salt and pepper and continue to sauté, until the peppers soften but still have a little crunch left, about 5 minutes. Add the cumin, saffron, and bell pepper puree. Simmer the mixture, adjusting the seasoning with salt, pepper, and sugar as it begins to thicken.

_____

Meanwhile, heat the remaining tablespoon of oil in a medium skillet over medium-high heat. Sauté the okra until golden, then add it to the pepper mixture. Add the tomato puree, a little bit at a time, until the ratatouille looks like a thickened stew (but not a soup). Add the nutmeg, cayenne, and lemon juice and reseason with salt, pepper, and sugar. Add the parsley and coriander and swirl in the butter.

PLATING

_____

Spoon the ratatouille into a large serving bowl. Serve accompanied by crisp, warm crêpes.

OUR TASTE NOTES

The bell peppers strike a bright garden note, assisted by the cumin and nutmeg. Coriander leaves and parsley are a light floral herbal counterpoint to the aromatic spices. Finally, the bean crêpe coats the palate, setting the stage for floral herbal, spiced aromatic, and garden tastes, softened by a hint of caramelized sweetness.

HONEY-GLAZED CELERY ROOT WITH A GINGER CURRY SAUCE

CELERY ROOT IS RARELY USED as a main ingredient but it should be. It is such a pleasingly crunchy vegetable with a taste both fruity and lightly bitter. This means it can focus other tastes that are much more powerful. The glaze and the ginger curry sauce here, for example, are strong but are persuaded to behave decorously by the celery root. You can also glaze beets, turnips, and squash and serve them with this emulsion.

SERVES 4 AS A SIDE DISH

GLAZE

2 tablespoons extra virgin olive oil
2 shallots, finely diced
¼ stalk lemongrass, thinly sliced
Zest of ½ lemon, julienned
¼ cup crystallized ginger
1 cup white port
½ cup red wine vinegar (we like sherry)
2 tablespoons honey
Kosher salt
Freshly ground white pepper

———

Heat the oil in a saucepan over medium-high heat. Add the shallots and sauté until golden. Add the lemongrass, lemon zest, and ginger and cook for 1 minute. Add the port and vinegar and simmer until reduced by one-third (a light syrup consistency).

———

Add the honey (watch how clear it gets), season with salt and pepper, and strain through a fine sieve. Return to the pan and keep warm over very low heat.

CELERY ROOT

1 large celery root, peeled and cut in ½-inch slices
2 tablespoons extra virgin olive oil
Kosher salt
Freshly ground white pepper

———

Preheat the oven to 350 degrees. Brush the celery root slices with oil and bake for 20 minutes. Season the celery root with salt and pepper and place under the broiler to brown the tops.

GARNISH

1 tablespoon butter
¼ cup julienned zucchini
¼ cup ½-inch chive lengths
Kosher salt

Melt the butter in a small skillet over medium-high heat. Add the zucchini and sauté for 2–3 minutes. Add the chives and season with salt.

SAUCE

1 cup Ginger Curry Sauce (page 228)

PLATING

———

Arrange the celery root on warm plates. Spoon glaze over each slice, garnish with zucchini and chives, and serve with Ginger Curry Sauce on the side.

OUR TASTE NOTES

The vinegar pulls out sweetness from the port and honey and accents the floral fruitiness in the port and the ginger. The curry sauce smoothes out the taste while the spiced aromatic curry re-introduces some edges to the flavor. The celery root has punctuating crunch as well as a little sharpness, which again focuses tastes. The final notes are tang, sweetness, and picante heat with spiced aromatic echoes to finish.

FLORAL HERBAL

FLUKE WITH SPICED CREAM OF WHEAT CRUST AND LEMON HERBAL BROTH

FLUKE, A MILD-MANNERED enough fish, becomes the base for a duet between a crisp, picante crust and tangy Lemon Herbal Broth. Serve this recipe with a freshly baked baguette (to sop up the liquid) and a green salad, and you have the makings of a terrific shore lunch. If you can't get to the shore, you can take a mouthful of this, close your eyes, and see where your thoughts take you.

SERVES 4

BROTH

⅔ cup extra virgin olive oil

2 tablespoons finely diced shallots

2 cloves garlic, thinly sliced

2 tablespoons chopped fresh thyme leaves

⅔ cup lemon juice

½ cup dry white vermouth

1 tablespoon sugar

Kosher salt

Freshly ground white pepper

Pinch cayenne pepper

2 tablespoons chopped fresh basil leaves

———

Heat the oil in a medium saucepan over medium-high heat. Add the shallots and garlic and cook, stirring occasionally, until lightly golden. Add the thyme, then the lemon juice, vermouth, sugar, salt, white pepper, and cayenne. (Keep tasting as you season and reseason. This light broth requires a lot of balancing before the tastes harmonize.) Add chopped basil just before serving.

CRUST AND FISH

1 egg plus 1 yolk, whisked together

4 teaspoons flour

½ teaspoon kosher salt

¼ teaspoon ground black pepper

4 6-ounce skinless fluke fillets (or other delicate white-fleshed fish)

About 1 cup Cream of Wheat and Cayenne Breading (see page 189)

About ¼ cup peanut or other neutral vegetable oil

———

Combine the egg and flour. Whisk until smooth. Whisk in seasoning. Dip each fillet first in the egg binding, then in the cream of wheat breading, shaking off any excess. Heat the oil in a skillet over medium-high heat. Fry the fish until golden brown on each side, about 2 minutes maximum per side. Drain on paper towels.

GARNISH

Zest of ¼ lemon, cut in julienne

¼ cup diced , seeded, and skinned tomato

PLATING

Place each fillet in the bottom of a wide bowl. Garnish with lemon julienne and tomato dice, then ladle the broth around the fish and serve.

OUR TASTE NOTES

The first notes are floral herbal. Then punctuation from the crunch of the fish. As you get into the flesh, the tang and light sweetness of the broth picks up added power from the cayenne's picante heat. The lemon zest and tomato have a pleasing texture while reinforcing the tangy acidity of the floral herbal broth. The fish serves to soften the attack of the broth and to extend the flavor as you chew.

CORN FENNEL CHOWDER WITH MUSSELS AND GRITS

THIS RECIPE UNITES two affinities of shellfish: the potatoes and creaminess of a New England clam chowder, and the herbs — especially the licorice-accented herbs — of a Provençal fish stew. In restaurants, corn is often served with cream or cream sauces, but it seemed that milk would work just as well in smoothing and rounding and picking up the sweet delicate corn taste. When the sous-chefs at Lespinasse used to gather around that particular stockpot to gab in the morning, you knew that you had an aroma that pleased.

SERVES 4

CORN AND POTATOES

6 ears corn, husks removed

1½ cups milk

8 pieces star anise

Kosher salt

1 tablespoon sugar

2 cups peeled medium-diced potatoes

————

Combine the corn, milk, star anise, 1 tablespoon salt and the sugar in a large pot. Add water to cover and bring to a boil. Cook until the corn is tender then remove it from the pot. Strain the liquid, reserving about 2 cups (to thin the soup if necessary). Remove the kernels from the cobs and set aside 3 cups for the chowder and the remainder for garnish.

————

Cook the potatoes in boiling salted water until tender, about 5 minutes. Reserve for garnish.

MUSSELS AND CHOWDER BASE

2 tablespoons butter

1 fennel bulb, trimmed (fronds reserved), cored, and chopped (approximately 2 cups)

1½ cups finely diced onions

2 tablespoons diced shallots

4 cloves garlic, peeled and crushed

5 or 6 sprigs fresh thyme

1 bay leaf

1 sprig fresh rosemary

4 dozen mussels

1½ cups dry white wine

2 cups water

¾ cup heavy cream

3 cups strained cooked corn liquid (see above)

Kosher salt

Freshly ground white pepper

Cayenne pepper

Juice of ½ lemon

⅓ cup Pernod

1 tablespoon instant grits

———

Melt the butter in a large pot over medium-high heat. Add the
fennel, onions, shallots, garlic, thyme, bay leaf, and rosemary and
cook until the fennel and onions are soft. Add the mussels, white
wine, and water. Bring to a boil and cook, removing the mussels as
they open. Discard those that don't.

———

Add the cream and the 3 cups of corn to the mussel cooking liquid.
Allow the mixture to return to a boil, then transfer to a food processor and puree. Strain the puree through a fine sieve, then return to
the pan and season with salt, pepper, cayenne, and lemon juice. Add
Pernod. Add the grits to the chowder and bring it back to a boil.
Thin the chowder, if necessary, with a little of the reserved corn
cooking liquid, then beat with an immersion blender (or whisk)
until frothy.

GARNISH

Cooked mussels (see above), shells removed and discarded

Reserved corn (see above)

Reserved potatoes (see above)

Reserved fennel fronds (see above)

1 bunch fresh tarragon

1 bunch fresh thyme

PLATING

———

Divide the mussels and corn among four wide soup plates.
Garnish with fennel fronds, tarragon, and thyme sprigs, then ladle
in chowder base and serve.

The milky broth is the first taste. It works in concert with the tarragon and Pernod, which give off a licorice floral herbal bouquet, that pulls sweetness up from the corn. Next, you get the crunch of the corn and its starchiness combines with the potato to clean the palate. The mussels have a buttery oceanic taste. Licorice, herbs, sweet creamy roundness, and shellfish persist in the finish.

MARINATED CRABMEAT WITH LIME MELON SAUCE

AT THE REGENT HOTEL in Hong Kong, customers often ordered melon juice. When the kitchen crew juiced the melons they would discard the pulp. But there was still an enormous amount of juice in the pulp. That kind of waste drives a chef to distraction, and it suggested the idea of reducing juice to create a sweet, powerful, yet light sauce and serving it with fresh cold seafood.

SERVES 4

SAUCE

1 cantaloupe, peeled and seeded

2 lemons, juiced

½ cup honey

2 teaspoons sugar

Kosher salt

Cayenne pepper

———

Roughly chop one-fourth of the cantaloupe and reserve for use in the salad (see below). Puree the remaining three-fourths in a blender or food processor. Strain the puree through a fine sieve, discarding the pulp. Heat the cantaloupe juice in a saucepan over medium heat. Add half the lemon juice and all the honey, and gently reduce until the juice is syrupy, about 10 minutes. Cool the syrup over ice. When well chilled, add the sugar and season with salt and cayenne and remaining lemon juice to taste. Reseason. Refrigerate until ready to use.

SHELLFISH SALAD

½ pound cooked crabmeat, picked through to remove hard bits

½ pound small, cooked shrimp, peeled and deveined

Reserved chopped cantaloupe (see above)

⅓ cup mint julienne

1 tablespoon white sesame seeds, toasted

2 lemons, juiced

2 limes, zested and juiced

⅛ cup grapeseed oil

3 drops sesame oil

Kosher salt

Freshly ground white pepper

Pinch sugar

Cayenne pepper

———

Combine the crab, shrimp, chopped cantaloupe, mint, and sesame seeds in a bowl and mix gently. Add the lemon and lime juices, grapeseed and sesame oils, and lime zest. Toss gently, then season with salt, pepper, sugar, and cayenne.

GARNISH

1 avocado, peeled, seeded, and cut in medium dice

¼ cup thinly sliced radishes

1 tablespoon chopped mint

½ cup taro chips (or Terra vegetable chips), broken up

PLATING

Place avocado in the center of four chilled plates. (We use a 6-inch ring mold to keep things tidy.) Top the avocado with shellfish salad, garnish with radishes, mint, and taro chips. Spoon the sauce around the molded salad.

OUR TASTE NOTES

The floral, fruity aroma of cantaloupe, citrus, and honey begins the taste. Next you find the crunch of the sesame seeds and the oceanic taste and texture of the shellfish. The avocados round the flavors, pulling out more of the fresh seafood. The tang of the citrus pulls the sweet fruit and seafood forward, while the zest and the mint pull up the floral side of the cantaloupe.

POACHED AND CRISPED TURKEY LEG
PROVENÇALE WITH LEMON PICKLE

WE CAME UP with this recipe for two reasons. First, we had an extra turkey leg lying around after we tested Turkey Leg in Chianti Topped with Pan-Roasted Winter Vegetables (page 70), and second, we felt that the approach here would be a way to lighten up what is normally thought of as a dense and heavy meat. It is a way to have turkey without going whole hog — or whole turkey.

SERVES 2

TURKEY

1 turkey leg (drumstick and thigh) from a 12-pound turkey

Kosher salt

Freshly ground white pepper

2 heads garlic cut in half (remove a few outer layers of skin)

1 leek, split and washed

1 sprig rosemary

15 sprigs thyme

1 bay leaf

1 cup dry vermouth

10 white peppercorns

1 tablespoon extra virgin olive oil

2 tablespoons grapeseed or other neutral vegetable oil

———

Season the turkey with salt and pepper and place in a large pot or Dutch oven. Add all of the remaining ingredients except the grapeseed oil. Add water to cover and a pinch of salt and bring to boil. Lower the heat to medium-low and simmer until the turkey is tender, about 2 hours (birds will vary, so check from time to time). Remove from the pot and pat dry. Strain the braising liquid through a coarse sieve, pressing the garlic through so that it enriches the broth. Return the broth to the pot and keep warm.

———

Just before serving, heat the grapeseed oil in a large skillet over high heat. Add the turkey and crisp the thigh, skin side only, about 5 minutes.

TOPPING

2 tablespoons extra virgin olive oil

1 shallot, thinly sliced

8 sun-dried tomatoes, cut in a medium julienne

1 teaspoon lavender flowers (optional, but if you can find them, we love them; spice stores and specialty catalogues often carry them)

½ Pickled Lemon (page 240), sliced

⅓ cup thinly sliced leeks

6–8 kalamata olives, pitted and thinly sliced

———

Heat the oil in a medium skillet over medium-high heat. Add the shallot and cook, stirring occasionally, until the shallot is soft and translucent. Add all the remaining ingredients and continue cooking for 3 minutes.

PLATING

———

Return the turkey to the pot, garnish with topping, and serve.

OUR TASTE NOTES

The first notes are floral herbal from the lavender and thyme which temper the intense meaty bouquet of the turkey. The garlic is sweetly bulby. The lemon adds a floral tang, while its soft texture leads to the tomatoes and the olives. The olives, in addition to salt, have a hint of floral. These are all light and bright tastes that the meat showcases. The end notes are meaty and tangy with an occasional floral herbal flourish.

HONEY LAVENDER WALLEYE

THIS COMES FROM one of the signature dishes at Lespinasse. The fish was skewered on lavender twigs and cooked on hot rocks. When the waiters brought it to the table, the whole room was bathed in a smoky, musky perfume. It was overpoweringly sensual. Try this with lavender skewers if you can find them. If not, grilling or barbecuing the fish without skewers is fine. You can strain some of the sauce and brush it on as a barbecue glaze on other fishes, even fresh fruits. It also makes a good sauce for desserts. As for the walleye, it is often touted by Midwesterners as the most delectable of fish. If you can't find or catch a walleye, then striped bass, halibut, and even cod will do.

SERVES 4

SAUCE

½ cup extra virgin olive oil
½ cup finely diced shallots
1 cup lemon juice
2 cups sweet white wine (sauterne, muscat, beaunes de venise)
1½ tablespoons honey
½ teaspoon dried lavender flowers (usually we recommend a substitute for hard-to-find ingredients; in this case, you need the flowers. Spice stores usually have them in stock and specialty food catalogues do, too)
Kosher salt
Freshly ground white pepper
Cayenne pepper

———

Heat 2 tablespoons of the oil in a medium skillet over medium-high heat. Add the shallots and sweat until they are soft. Add the lemon juice and wine, bring to a boil, and reduce by about three-fourths (to a syrup). Add the honey, the lavender flowers, and the remaining oil. Season with salt, pepper, and cayenne. Keep warm.

TOPPING

1 tablespoon butter
1 tablespoon olive oil
½ cup slivered almonds, toasted
¼ cup finely diced shallots
Zest of 1 lemon, julienned
⅓ cup finely chopped parsley
½ teaspoon dried lavender flowers (reserve)

———

Heat the butter and oil in the skillet over medium-high heat. Add the shallots and cook, stirring occasionally, until golden, then season with salt. Add the almonds and lemon zest and heat over low. Just before serving, add fresh chopped parsley.

WALLEYE

4 6-ounce walleye fillets (or other firm white-fleshed fish — i.e., no fluke or flounder)

Kosher salt

Freshly ground white pepper

2 tablespoons extra virgin olive oil

———

Season the fish with salt and pepper. Film a large skillet with oil and pan-roast the fish until it is golden on both sides and warm at the center, no more than 2 minutes on each side for average walleye. If you use other fish, thickness will vary and so will cooking time.

PLATING

———

Spoon sauce onto four plates, place a fillet on each plate, garnish with topping and lavender flowers, and serve.

OUR TASTE NOTES

The first note, and it is a strong one, is floral — mostly from the lavender flowers but assisted by the honey, olive oil, and lemon. The sweetness of the honey and the tang of the lemon are punctuated by the topping's crunch. The bulby shallots bring up more floral herbal and open up the palate to sweetness. The fish gives texture and an oceanic taste. The last notes are sweet fruitiness, a floral nose, and picante heat.

FUNKY

THE OPPOSITE OF PRIMAVERA—TRUFFLED
SPAGHETTI SQUASH AND LATE GARDEN VEGETABLES

HERE WE HAVE TRUFFLES, wine, cream — all things that often are served with pasta. We lightened it with a medley of fall vegetables anchored by spaghetti squash. At least that is what our method looks like in retrospect. Actually we opened the refrigerator at the Kunz apartment and most of the ingredients were there already (okay we admit it, chefs sometimes have truffles lying around). It was a cold nasty day when neither of us wanted to go marketing, so we cooked with what we had.

SERVES 4 AS A SIDE DISH

INGREDIENTS

2 spaghetti squash, halved

3 tablespoons butter

Kosher salt

Freshly ground white pepper

1 shallot, finely diced

¼ cup julienne of celery root

1½ ounces black truffles, chopped (optional)

¼ cup heavy cream

¼ cup julienned butternut squash

¼ cup dry white wine

1 cup chopped parsley

———

Preheat the oven to 375 degrees. Place the spaghetti squash, split side up, in a roasting pan. Dot the squash with half the butter, season with salt and pepper, then roast until a forkful of squash separates like strands of pasta, about 40 minutes. Remove the squash from the oven and spoon out the "spaghetti." Set aside.

———

Melt the remaining butter in a high-sided skillet over medium-high heat. Add the shallots and celery root and cook until they just begin to soften, about 1 minute, then add the truffles. Cook for about 1 minute more, then add the cream, spaghetti squash, julienne of butternut squash, and wine. Bring the mixture to a boil, adjust the seasoning with salt and pepper, then serve garnished with parsley.

OUR TASTE NOTES

The shallot opens the bouquet then the floral herbal parsley moves the taste toward the garden crunch of the squash and celery root. By contrast, the cream reinforces the wintry earthiness in the celery root and funkiness in the truffle. The squash has garden vegetable taste, and background sweetness. The cream also picks up picante and spiced aromatic tones. The last notes are roundness from the cream and truffle perfume.

DAVID CUNNINGHAM, who was a sous-chef at Lespinasse and is now the chef at Petrossian in Manhattan, is also the leader of a bagpipe band and a Korean food aficionado. One day he took us to a former bar mitzvah/wedding palace near Shea Stadium that has since become a Korean restaurant. It is also a 24-hour restaurant favored by many of New York's Korean grocers and fish shop owners. To test our commitment as gourmets, David ordered white kimchee (fermented cabbage) stewed with pork bellies and served with raw oysters. Although we liked it, we will not ask the reader to go that extra experimental mile. However, oysters and cabbage turned out to be a nice autumn combination, and here is the result.

SERVES 4 AS AN APPETIZER

SAUCE

1 cup warm Aromatic Mustard Sauce (page 229)

CABBAGE

2 cups finely sliced napa-type (Chinese) cabbage
Kosher salt
2 tablespoons butter
Freshly ground white pepper

————

Blanch the cabbage for 2 minutes in boiling salted water. Shock it in cold water, then squeeze as dry as possible.

————

Melt the butter in a large skillet over medium-high heat. Add the blanched cabbage, season with salt and pepper, and cook, stirring occasionally, until the cabbage is soft to the bite, approximately 3–4 minutes for a young tender cabbage. Keep warm.

OYSTERS

1 egg plus 1 yolk, whisked together
¼ cup flour
½ teaspoon kosher salt
¼ teaspoon ground black pepper
2 dozen shelled oysters, drained and patted dry
1 cup bread crumbs
About ½ cup corn or other neutral vegetable oil
Kosher salt

————

Combine the egg and flour. Whisk until smooth, then whisk in the seasoning. Coat the oysters first with the binding, then the bread crumbs, shaking off any excess. Heat oil over medium-high heat until it is good and hot. Fry the oysters, a few at a time, until golden, about 15 seconds per side. Drain on paper towels and sprinkle with salt.

PLATING

Mound cabbage in the center of four plates. Spoon sauce around the cabbage, then top with oysters and serve.

OUR TASTE NOTES

The mustard sauce begins with a sharp tang. The cabbage, too, has a little sharpness, but its overall effect is a smooth texture. It leads into the crunch of the breading and then the softness of the oyster. The funkiness in the cabbage pulls out the bouquet of the oyster. The celery root in the sauce also adds crunch, which makes for good contrast to the smooth oyster. The last note is spiced aromatic from the cumin in the sauce. It pulls all of the soft subtle flavors of the oyster forward.

APPLE, BRUSSELS SPROUT, AND TURNIP HASH

THERE HAS PROBABLY NEVER BEEN an Earthling child who was born liking brussels sprouts, and if such a child exists you can be sure that turnips aren't high on his or her culinary agenda. But they are so good. The problem is how to prepare them in a way that even a kid will like them. Our kids liked this.

SERVES 4 AS A SIDE DISH

INGREDIENTS

½ pound brussels sprouts, quartered

Kosher salt

3½ tablespoons butter

2 Granny Smith apples, peeled, cored, and sliced

¼ cup plus 1 tablespoon cider vinegar

1 large white turnip, peeled and cut into ¼-inch dice

8–10 slices crumbled crisped bacon

Freshly ground white pepper

Pinch sugar

––––––

Blanch the brussels sprouts in boiling salted water, about 2 minutes, then drain and shock in cold water.

––––––

Melt 1½ tablespoons of butter in a large skillet over medium-high heat. Add the brussels sprouts and cook, stirring occasionally until they begin to brown, about 5 minutes. Remove the brussels sprouts from the pan and set aside. Add 1 tablespoon of the remaining butter and the apples and cook until they are golden, 4–5 minutes. Set the apples aside.

––––––

Bring ¼ cup of vinegar to a boil. Add the turnips, season with salt, then simmer until the turnips are tender and the vinegar reduced by half. Add the brussels sprouts to the turnips and continue to reduce for 2–3 minutes. Just before serving, add the apples, heat through, then add the remaining butter and crisped bacon. Adjust the seasoning with vinegar, sugar, and salt, and serve.

OUR TASTE NOTES

Sweetness combines with funkiness for a broad, powerful taste. The first note is funky earthiness from the brussels sprouts, softened by the apple's fruity aroma. The turnips, through bitterness, help punctuate and focus. The vinegar brightens the very broad tastes and the bacon has a funky aged bouquet while adding salt. The last notes are salt, funk, and sweetness.

TASTES THAT PUNCTUATE

Their chief function is

to disseminate taste,

spreading it on the palate

and launching it, as

aroma, into the nose.

SHARP/BITTER

KALE SIMMERED WITH FAT-
BACK and sugar is a soul food
staple. The bitterness of the kale
stands up to the rich smoky
sweetness of salt pork favored in
Southern cooking. We chose to
get our saltiness from soy sauce,
and once headed in that Asian
direction we added in ginger. This
combination works with watercress, another bitter green. We
haven't tried it with collards or
mustard greens, but it should
work equally well with them.

SERVES 4

INGREDIENTS

1 pound kale, chopped roughly into 1½-inch pieces

Kosher salt

2 tablespoons grapeseed or other neutral vegetable oil

1 tablespoon grated ginger

½ red bell pepper, seeded and sliced

3 tablespoons soy sauce

Freshly ground white pepper

Pinch sugar

———

Cook the kale in a large pot of boiling salted water, stirring occasionally, until the stems are almost cooked—they will still have a
slight crunch—about 6–8 minutes. Drain the kale, shock it in cold
water, then dry well (this is easiest in a salad spinner).

———

Heat the oil in a large skillet over medium-high heat. Add the ginger
and peppers and cook until they begin to soften, 2–3 minutes. Add
the kale and cook until it is warm. Add the soy sauce, adjust the
seasoning with salt, pepper, and sugar, and serve.

OUR TASTE NOTES

The floral ginger and the sugar highlight the sweet side of the bell
pepper. The salty soy sauce pushes the fresh garden taste of the bell
pepper and brings out the garden aspect of the kale. The kale has a
slight crunch, and its bitterness keeps the other tastes focused and
distinct. This dish would probably not be served alone, so it would
be tasted only in context of something rich and powerful like a
glazed duck, where its bitterness goes to work punctuating another
huge taste.

SAUSAGE WITH LAGER SAUCE AND APPLE BOUILLON

AT ANY ITALIAN STREET FAIR, you can buy sausages with mounds of caramelized onions that brown up in the sizzling fat rendered by the sausages. At any football tailgating party you can rest assured that someone will be eating brats (as in bratwurst) and beer: ice-cold, palate-cleansing, bitter beer. So it doesn't seem like a stretch, then, to combine these tastes in one dish. With all that meaty, bulby, salty, bitter interaction going on we knew we could raise the taste level with the fruity tang of an apple cider bouillon.

SERVES 4

BOUILLON

2 cups apple cider
⅓ cup cider or rice vinegar
1 tablespoon sugar
¼ teaspoon ground cloves
¼ teaspoon ground cinnamon
Kosher salt
Pinch cayenne pepper

———

Combine all of the ingredients except the salt and cayenne in a saucepan. Bring the mixture to a boil, then reduce the heat and simmer for 5 minutes. (You are not trying to create a reduction. You simply want to extract flavor.) Strain the bouillon through a sieve lined with a coffee filter, then season with salt and cayenne. Keep warm over very low heat.

SAUSAGE AND ONIONS

8 links Italian sausage
2 cups finely sliced onion
4 cups lager beer
1 tablespoon flour

———

Combine the sausages, onions, and 2 cups of the lager in a high-sided skillet. Bring to a boil then reduce the heat and simmer until the juices evaporate and pan is dry and the sausages are nicely browned all over. Remove the sausages from the pan and set aside. Stir the flour into the onions, then deglaze with the remaining 2 cups of beer, scraping up any bits sticking to the pan bottom. Simmer the mixture for 2 minutes.

PLATING

———

Divide the sausages among four wide soup plates. Top with thickened onion-lager mixture, surround with bouillon, and serve.

OUR TASTE NOTES

The strong meatiness from the sausage gives off a full aroma that is pulled up by the bulbiness of the onion. The lightly bitter note from the beer cuts the meaty heaviness. The sweetness and tang of the bouillon balance the bitterness of the beer.

HAM HOCKS AND SPARERIBS IN CHERRY BEER

IN BRAISING, separate tastes tend to get suffused into a larger, subtle mix: flavors emerge like wisps of smoke and evanesce into the warm braising liquid. Here we combine meats—fatty spareribs and smoky ham hocks—and we braise them in a cherry beer inspired by the homeland of Lespinasse colleague Fabrizzio Salerni. The bitterness of the beer, counterbalanced by the fruity cherry, works on the intense meatiness of the pork. Everything else that we added to this recipe is an example of taste encountering new taste, point and counterpoint in order to round, mellow, deepen those basic tastes. Since you are not cooking in a restaurant kitchen presided over by a super-strict chef, you might as well enjoy a bottle of cherry beer while you cook.

SERVES 4

HAM HOCKS

2 tablespoons corn oil

4 smoked ham hocks

2–3 pounds (depending on your appetite) pork spareribs, country style

1 medium carrot, peeled and cut into 1-inch lengths

1 large leek, white part only, cut into 1-inch lengths

1 large stalk celery, cut into 1-inch lengths

1 large onion, peeled and diced

6 cloves garlic (left whole)

1 small bunch rosemary, tied with a string

3 bay leaves

6 cloves

10 peppercorns

2 teaspoons tomato paste

⅓ cup flour

3 cups cherry beer (or lager beer mixed with 2 tablespoons cherry preserves)

2 cups water

Kosher salt

Freshly ground white pepper

Pinch sugar

———

Preheat the oven to 350 degrees. Heat the oil in a large heavy pot over medium-high heat. Add the hocks and ribs and brown them on all sides, about 5 minutes. Remove the meat and add the carrot, leek, celery, onion, garlic, herbs, and peppercorns. Cook until well browned, then add the tomato paste and flour. Cook, stirring frequently, for 3–4 minutes. Deglaze with beer, scraping up the bits on the bottom, then return the hocks and ribs to the pot and add the water. Bring to a boil, then cover and transfer to the oven. Cook until the hocks and ribs are very tender, 2–2½ hours. Taste the braising liquid, add more beer to taste, and adjust the seasoning with salt, pepper, and sugar, then keep warm in the covered pot until ready to serve. Strain and remove fat from the cooking liquid and return to pot with vegetables and ribs.

CABBAGE

1 head green cabbage, core removed and leaves separated

Kosher salt

2 tablespoons butter

Freshly ground white pepper

¼ cup chopped tarragon

———

Blanch the cabbage leaves in a large pot of boiling salted water, approximately 3 minutes. Drain them, then shock in cold water. Melt the butter in a large skillet over medium heat. Add the cabbage, season with salt and pepper, and cook until soft, 2–3 minutes. Remove the pan from the heat. Add the tarragon and adjust the seasoning with salt and pepper.

PLATING

———

Place the hocks, ribs, and braising vegetables on a platter. Arrange the cabbage around the meat, then ladle braising liquid over meat and vegetables. Top with Onion, Horseradish, Apple Topping (optional).

OUR TASTE NOTES

Intense meatiness and funky smokiness come through first. Horseradish, mustard, cabbage, and peppercorns all tend to focus and punctuate the meat. The onions open the bouquet and prepare the palate to receive the sweetness of the apples. The butter and mustard round the tastes. The licorice in the tarragon pulls up both sweetness and meatiness. The fundamental bitterness and sharpness from the beer and the horseradish sound a single clear note in the topping.

WILTED ENDIVES, CRANBERRIES, AND YAMS

THERE IS BITTER all over this recipe—you have bitter endive, bitter in the almonds, and bitter in the cranberries—but when all is said and done, it is not a bitter dish. Instead, the bitterness in every case allies with a sweet, tangy, or salty component. The resulting mix will work well on the different components in another complex recipe like our Oven Crisped Chicken (page 156). The point is, bitter never stands alone. It is a taste that always needs a context in which to work, but given that context, it works like a charm.

SERVES 4

INGREDIENTS

6 endives, cut in ½-inch rounds, trimmed and rinsed
Juice of 1½ lemons
1 teaspoon kosher salt
1 tablespoon corn or other neutral vegetable oil
2 tablespoons sugar
3 tablespoons butter
½ medium yam, peeled and cut in a fine julienne
⅓ cup cranberries

———

Toss the endive slices, half the lemon juice, the salt, oil, and sugar together in a bowl.

———

Melt 1 tablespoon of the butter in a high-sided skillet over medium-high heat. Add the endive mixture, stir to coat with butter, then cover. Cook 2–3 minutes, lifting the cover to stir once or twice. Add the yams and cranberries. Cook 3–4 minutes, then add the remaining 2 tablespoons butter. Reseason with the remaining lemon juice and additional salt and sugar if necessary, then serve.

OUR TASTE NOTES

The butter and sugar give off a sweet and fruity apple pie smell. The endives and yams provide texture and crunch. The cranberries are tangy, sweet, and bitter, all at once. The bitter in the fruit works well with the bitter in the endives. The lemon reinforces the cranberry tang. The butter rounds out the distinct tastes and melds them. A sweet aroma persists at the close.

TASTE PLATFORMS

All platform ingredients
have a textural element,
which is a key, though
often overlooked,
component in the
taste process.

GARDEN

SHORT OF PUTTING THE WHOLE GARDEN in the food processor, there is no recipe that captures the flavors of summer herbs and vegetables better than this. You can use regular basil, but if you can find opal basil, its purple leaves give great color and a cinnamony flavor. The principle here is to get a narrow spectrum of similar ingredients to heighten the taste. One serving note: everything needs to be served cold. The ingredients are cold and the plates should be too.

SERVES 4

COULIS

2 pounds very ripe yellow cherry tomatoes, stems removed
2 pounds very ripe red cherry tomatoes, stems removed
Kosher salt
Freshly ground white pepper
Sugar

———

Slice enough yellow tomatoes to yield 1 cup and set aside for garnish. Puree each color tomato separately in a blender, then strain through a fine sieve into separate bowls. Chill (in a bowl over ice). Season each puree liberally with salt, pepper, and sugar, then chill. Before serving, pulse coulis lightly in a blender to create a foamy appearance and adjust the seasoning. Keep seasoning and tasting for balance.

GARNISH

Kosher salt
Freshly ground pepper
2 tablespoons extra virgin olive oil
2 tablespoons julienne of green basil leaves cut into small squares,
 ¼ × ¼ inch
½ tablespoon finely chopped thyme
1 tablespoon opal basil flowers (optional)
1 tablespoon julienne of opal basil
⅓ cup bush basil on stem

PLATING

———

In two steady streams, simultaneously pour red and yellow purees into chilled soup bowls. (They will stay separate for a yin-yang look.) Garnish with sliced tomatoes, basil squares, thyme, and basil flowers (if using) in each bowl, then mound julienne of opal basil in the center. Top with basil sprigs and serve.

The frothiness of the tomatoes delivers clear garden notes, heightened by the complex floral herbal aroma of the basil flowers. Salt develops and pushes these flavors. The tang of the tomatoes pulls out more flavor, while its smoothness delivers a texture that rounds out the angles of the taste. The final notes are tangy, sweet, and picante.

GRATIN OF SWEET PEAS, TARRAGON, AND PISTACHIOS

THIS STARTED FROM A VISION rather than a taste: a composition of peas, pistachio, and tarragon—all green. Peas have garden vegetable taste. The tarragon, with its licorice aroma, will pull up sweetness in peas. Then we added some Riesling for tang and sweetness. Gratin refers to putting something under the broiler to brown the top. The caramelization creates crunch and a sweet nutty aroma.

SERVES 4 AS A SIDE DISH

INGREDIENTS

1 cup heavy cream

2 cups shucked peas

Kosher salt

1 tablespoon butter

2 tablespoons chopped shallots

¾ cup Riesling

⅓ cup shelled pistachios, toasted and salted

¼ cup chopped tarragon

24 pea shoots (or 12 baby spinach leaves)

———

Whip ⅓ cup cream to firm peaks then refrigerate.

———

Blanch the peas in salted boiling water for 2 minutes. Drain and shock in ice water. Drain and set aside.

———

Melt the butter in a large skillet over medium heat. Add the shallots and cook until translucent. Add the Riesling, bring to a boil, and reduce by one-third. Add the remaining cream and simmer until it is thick enough to coat the back of a wooden spoon. Add the peas and pistachios and bring to boil. Very gently fold in the whipped cream. Transfer the mixture to a heatproof serving dish. Gratinee (brown the top) under a preheated broiler (this happens very quickly, so take care not to burn). Garnish with remaining herbs and greens.

OUR TASTE NOTES

The licoricey floral herbal bouquet of the tarragon pulls up the sweet roundness of the cream. Next, you find the garden crunch of the peas and the nutty crunch of pistachios. The Riesling accents the garden vegetable taste and adds a sweetness and a tanginess that focuses the palate.

MAY RAGOUT OF MORELS, GARDEN SHOOTS, AND GREENS

MORELS ARE THE SUREST SIGN that cold weather is kaput. When the morels first show, the leaves have the light green blush of budding youth. By the time the morels have come and gone, the forest is in full leaf. Morels, cream, and Madeira are the essence of soft earthy sweetness. Paired with the first vegetables of early spring, this combination says good-bye to winter and hello to vegetables that have just pushed through the same sun-warmed earth that sends forth morels.

SERVES 4 AS AN APPETIZER

POTATOES AND BROTH

2 small fingerling (or other early spring) potatoes, peeled
About 1 cup chicken stock
1 clove garlic
1 bay leaf

———

Cut the potatoes into quarters. Combine the potatoes, stock, garlic, and bay leaf in a saucepan and simmer gently until the potatoes are tender (the time will depend on the type of potatoes). Drain the potatoes, reserving the liquid. Set the potatoes aside.

MORELS

3 cups fresh morels
1 tablespoon butter
1 shallot, finely diced
Kosher salt
Freshly ground white pepper
½ cup Madeira
1–1⅓ cups heavy cream

———

Just before cooking, spray the morels thoroughly with water. (Use the sprayer on your kitchen sink—you don't want the mushrooms to absorb too much water, so do this at the last minute.) Blot the morels dry with a towel or spin them in a salad spinner. Trim the bottoms and split the large morels lengthwise in half.

———

Melt the butter in a large skillet over medium-high heat, add the shallots, and cook, stirring, until they are translucent. Add the morels, season with salt and pepper, and cook until the morels soften, 3–4 minutes (depending on the size of the morels and how moist they are). Add the Madeira, then 1 cup of cream, then the potatoes. Simmer until the cream coats the back of a wooden spoon. (The cream will thicken up very quickly; adjust the thickness with the reserved potato liquid.) Finish with another ⅓ cup of cream if desired.

GARNISH

15–20 small breakfast radishes (or other small radishes), halved
    lengthwise
1 cup pea shoots
1 cup baby spinach leaves
8–10 sorrel leaves

————

NOTE: If you can't find the pea shoots, or spinach, or sorrel, don't
worry. Substitute a combination of sautéed young asparagus tops
and tangy young greens or herbs. The idea is to add a little crunch,
a little tang, and a little green freshness.

PLATING

————

Ladle the morel ragout into warm soup bowls. Garnish with
radishes, pea shoots, and greens and serve.

OUR TASTE NOTES

The shallots open the bouquet, pulling up the morels and potatoes.
The pea shoots have a garden crunch. The spinach, lightly bitter,
keeps the Madeira cream from overwhelming the palate. The sorrel's tang focuses these broad tastes, while the radishes contribute
sharpness and crunch. The morels have both a silky texture and a
beautiful and delicate earthiness. The last note is the sweet roundness of the cream.

BRAISED CARDOONS WITH CRISP BACON, ONIONS, AND POTATOES

CARDOONS, TRADITIONALLY STORED in a root cellar, are for many French and Italian farm families the last garden vegetable of the season. Italian markets often have them around Christmastime. They have elements of the crunch and lightness of summer vegetables with the almost starchy taste of wintry vegetables. Think of the taste of cardoons as the child of a marriage between artichokes and celery. The great Freddy Girardet, the father (or more accurately, the benevolent uncle) of many of these recipes, was often deluged with requests for his truffles and cardoons.

SERVES 4 AS A SIDE DISH

INGREDIENTS

6 new potatoes, peeled and cut in half

Kosher salt

1 medium bunch cardoons, trimmed and deveined (this is a chore, but necessary; it is like removing veins from celery)

15 cippolini onions (or pearl onions), blanched and peeled

2 tablespoons roughly diced shallots

2 tablespoons flour

3 cups dry white wine

1 cup water

Juice of 1 lemon

2 tablespoons butter

Freshly ground white pepper

4 slices bacon, crisped and crumbled

———

Bring the potatoes to a boil in salted water and cook until almost, but not quite, tender. Drain and set aside. Meanwhile, prepare the cardoons.

———

Heat the oil in a large Dutch oven or braising pan over medium-high heat. Add the onions and cook until lightly caramelized, 3–4 minutes. Add the shallots and caramelize. Add the flour. Cook, stirring, until it is fragrant, 1–2 minutes more, then add the wine and water. Bring to a simmer, then add the cardoons and lemon juice. Reduce the heat to medium and braise until the cardoons are tender, approximately 40 minutes. Add the parboiled potatoes and butter, season with salt and pepper, and cook, until the potatoes are fully tender, another 5 minutes or so. Garnish with bacon and serve in the braising pan.

Cardoon is a very difficult taste to locate on the palate. It is an enabler in the same way that turmeric enables aromatic spices. Whatever it is that cardoons do, they start this dish with a smooth, garden bouquet. At the same time, the bulby onions pull up deeper flavor in the braised ingredients. The cardoons have celery-like garden crunch and their earthy undertones marry well with the aged salty bacon. The potatoes add smoothness. The wine and lemon juice focus tastes, which would otherwise become blurred and indistinct.

SUMMER SQUASH WITH TOMATO AND CHEDDAR IN CHARDONNAY, LEMON THYME EMULSION

COLD DIMINISHES TASTE.
Heat exaggerates it. By combining
a hot and cold treatment of the
same main ingredient, you create
a dynamic tension on the palate.
In addition to those two aspects
of the ingredient, we cook the
zucchini and chop it in different
ways: this gives us simultaneous
looks at all the taste possibilities
of this ingredient. Think of it as
culinary cubism. The Chardonnay,
lemon thyme emulsion is a
sweet variation on the classic
combination of lemons and
herbs. It also works with most
grilled vegetables, salty oven-
roasted vegetables, and grilled
shellfish.

SERVES 4

EMULSION

½ cup dry white wine

1 tablespoon sugar

Juice of ½ lemon

1 teaspoon lemon thyme leaves (if you cannot find lemon thyme
then use ½ tablespoon regular thyme and 1 teaspoon julienne
of lemon zest)

1 tablespoon extra virgin olive oil

Kosher salt

_____

Combine the wine, sugar, lemon juice, and half the thyme leaves in a
medium saucepan. Heat over medium-high heat until the mixture is
fragrant but not yet simmering. Add the oil and beat with an emulsion blender (or whisk vigorously). Add the remaining thyme, season
with salt, and keep warm over very low heat.

VEGETABLE STEW

4 round zucchinis or 2 small long zucchinis

3 tablespoons extra virgin olive oil

1 shallot, thinly sliced

1 clove garlic, thinly sliced

2 cups chopped, seeded tomato

Kosher salt

Freshly ground white pepper

1 tablespoon polenta or fine cornmeal

⅓ cup grated cheddar cheese

⅓ cup fresh tarragon, measured loose then roughly chopped

⅓ cup fresh parsley, measured first then roughly chopped

2 tablespoons lemon thyme leaves (or 2 tablespoons regular thyme
and minced zest of ½ lemon)

2 tablespoons balsamic vinegar

1 tablespoon red wine vinegar

If you are using round zucchini, cut off the ends and set them aside for garnish. Scoop out the flesh and seeds and reserve. If you are using long zucchini, cut them in half lengthwise then scoop out the soft inner flesh. Cut the scooped-out zucchini shells in half on an angle (you should have four shells about the same length) and set aside.

———

Heat half the oil in a large skillet over medium-high heat. Add the shallot and garlic and cook until fragrant. Add the zucchini pulp and cook until mushy, about 6–7 minutes, then add the tomatoes and season with salt and pepper. Lower the heat and simmer for 6–8 minutes. Stir in the polenta and simmer gently, stirring occasionally, until the vegetable mixture thickens slightly. Set aside to cool for about 20 minutes. Adjust the seasoning with salt and pepper.

———

Meanwhile, place the scooped-out zucchini skins in an oiled baking dish and preheat the oven to 450 degrees. Sprinkle two-thirds of the cheese then the tarragon and parsley in the bottom of each hollowed zucchini. Season the cheese and herb mixture with salt and pepper, then loosely fill the zucchini shells with the vegetable stew. Reserve the remaining stew for vegetable-vinaigrette garnish (see below). Top each stuffed zucchini with a bit more cheese and drizzle with about 1 tablespoon of olive oil, then transfer to the oven and bake for 12-15 minutes. Reduce the temperature to 300 degrees and continue baking until the zucchini skins are tender, 6–8 minutes more.

———

While the stuffed zucchini are baking, season the remaining vegetable stew with salt, pepper, and both vinegars. If you are using round zucchini, heat the remaining tablespoon of oil in a skillet over medium-high heat and add the reserved zucchini tops and pan-roast until crisp and golden. (Omit this step if you are using long zucchini.)

PLATING

———

Arrange the vegetables vinaigrette in the center of four plates
(we like to use a ring mold). Spoon the Chardonnay, Lemon
Thyme Emulsion around the molded vegetables, then place the
stuffed zucchini on top. Garnish with the crisped zucchini tops
(if using) and lemon thyme leaves.

OUR TASTE NOTES

As you spoon into the stuffing, you pick up a watery garden taste
from the zucchini, floral herbal notes from the herbs, and light
picante heat from the white pepper. The cheese rounds the tastes,
and the tarragon pulls up the zucchini's sweetness. The vinaigrette
in the salad pulls bright garden taste from the tomatoes and peppers. The contrast between the warm stuffing and the cool salad in
the base is bridged by the floral sweetness in the emulsion.

MEATY

STEAK TARTARE WITH PICKLED PAPAYA AND KETJAP MANIS

STEAK TARTARE IS A STAN-
DARD in the apprentice chef's
repertoire. But long years of making it exactly the same way have
led to a very predictable dish. The
addition of a few bright tastes,
however, wakes it right up. Regular
old ketchup, and a sweet Indonesian soy sauce–based condiment
called ketjap manis—available in
many Asian stores—proved to be
the secret ingredients here. The
pickled papaya doubles the tart
and sweet contribution of the
ketchup.

SERVES 4

INGREDIENTS

1½ pounds rump steak (or, if you want to get fancy, filet mignon)
¼ cup capers, finely chopped
⅛ cup finely diced shallots
1 egg yolk
⅓ cup finely chopped chives
½ cup chopped parsley
¼ cup tomato ketchup
¼ cup extra virgin olive oil
¼ cup brandy
½ cup diced jicama
Kosher salt
Freshly ground white pepper
½ teaspoon cayenne pepper
2 tablespoons Kunz Ketjap (page 226)
Toast points

_____

Chop the beef finely. Chill the chopped beef as you work, in a stainless-
steel bowl, over ice. Add the capers, shallots, egg yolk, chives, parsley,
tomato ketchup, olive oil, brandy, and jicama. Mix with a fork. Season
liberally with salt, lots of pepper, and cayenne. Now season some more
for good measure.

PLATING

_____

Form the steak tartare into four patties and set on chilled plates.
Make a depression in the center of each tartare, and drizzle with
ketjap manis. Garnish with additional chopped fresh herbs if desired,
and serve with croutons or toast points.

OUR TASTE NOTES

This is a very complex-tasting dish. The cumin in the ketjap manis pulls
up the capers and lemon juice. Their tang and the shallot's sweetness
pull out the garden fruitiness of ketchup. Brandy adds to the bouquet,
pulling up the lemon. The meat coats the palate and rounds the tastes.
The sharp chives punctuate and begin to close down the palate.

MARINATING AND BRAISING combine two methods of infusing and developing deep layers of flavor. Although the ingredient list looks a little long, you have our assurance that this is a pared down version of a much longer Lespinasse recipe. The fruity, acid marinade/braising liquid gives great definition to the soft, slow-cooked lamb. This marinade showcases the meat rather than hiding it as often happens with a classic brown sauce. Honey and mustard balance one another in smoothing the meat and refreshing the palate. Serve with Lentil Stew (page 181).

SERVES 4

MARINADE

¾ cup carrots in thick (½ inch) rounds

¼ cup roughly chopped celery root

1 large onion, diced

¼ cup roughly chopped peeled ginger

1 large leek, split

8 cloves garlic, left whole

2 shallots, roughly cut

3 cloves

1 tablespoon ground cumin

½ tablespoon ground mace

½ tablespoon whole black peppercorns

1 medium bunch thyme

1 small bunch rosemary

4 cups crushed tomatoes

4 cups dry white wine

½ cup lemon juice

———

Combine all of the ingredients in a large bowl.

LAMB

4 lamb shanks

Marinade (see above)

Kosher salt

Freshly ground white pepper

2 tablespoons grapeseed or other neutral vegetable oil

2 tablespoons flour

2 cups water

———

Coat the shanks with the marinade and refrigerate for one to two days.

———

Drain the shanks and the marinade vegetables, reserving the liquid. Bring the liquid to a boil in a saucepan, then strain through cheesecloth. Set aside.

Preheat the oven to 275 degrees. Season the shanks with salt and pepper. Heat the oil in a Dutch oven or braising pan over medium-high heat. Add the shanks and brown on all sides, 8 minutes. Remove and set aside. Next, caramelize the vegetables, cooking until browned and tender. Add the flour, and mix to coat the vegetables. Deglaze with the boiled marinade liquid, then return the shanks to the pan. Bring to a simmer, cover, and braise in the oven until the lamb is very tender, about 3½ hours. Add water if it has reduced too much. Remove the shanks and cover with aluminum foil to keep warm. Strain the braising liquid through a sieve, pressing the vegetables so that they thicken up the liquid. Degrease and reserve.

SAUCE

Strained braising liquid (see above)

3 tablespoons prepared mustard

2 tablespoons honey (eucalyptus if available)

2 tablespoons butter

Kosher salt

Freshly ground white pepper

2 tablespoons ramp juice from Pickled Ramps (page 242)
   (or 2 tablespoons white vinegar with 1 teaspoon sugar)

———

Heat the braising liquid in a saucepan over low heat. Add the mustard, honey, and butter and beat with an immersion blender (or whisk) until frothy. Add salt, pepper, and finish with pickling juice to taste. Beat or whisk again and keep warm.

TOPPING

2 tablespoons extra virgin olive oil

½ cup apricot almonds (the roasted pits of apricots, available in
   Middle Eastern stores, or substitute whole roasted almonds)

Kosher salt

Freshly ground white pepper

2 tablespoons dried homemade bread crumbs

5 sprigs of thyme, picked

½ cup chopped dried apricots

½ cup Pickled Ramps (page 242) (if ramps are not available, use scallions braised in white vinegar and sugar)

⅓ cup mint, roughly chopped then measured

⅓ cup chopped chives

⅓ cup parsley, roughly chopped then measured

2 tablespoons butter

———

Heat the oil in a medium skillet over medium-high heat. Add the almonds, season with salt and pepper, and roast until fragrant. Add the bread crumbs and cook until golden, then add the thyme and a bit more salt and pepper.

———

In another pan, heat the chopped apricots with the pickled ramps over medium heat. Swirl in the butter.

PLATING

———

Place lentil stew in the bottom of four wide soup plates. Place a lamb shank in each. Spoon sauce over the shanks and lentils. Top with apricot-almond-ramp mixture. Garnish with mint, chives, and parsley if desired, then serve.

OUR TASTE NOTES

The deep meatiness of this dish is a platform that supports everything else. There is a slight floral herbal perfume at the outset. This leads into the sharp and tangy pickling juice which, with the spices, focuses the palate. The ramps are sharp and bulby, so they pull up meatiness and punctuate it. The almonds add crunch, which again punctuates, and also adds a light bitterness. The result is that the unctuous meat is contained, and comes on in waves of flavor.

BRAISED OXTAIL WITH WINE
SAUCE REDUCTION

THE NEXT TIME you see some cattle grazing in a field, check out which muscle gets the biggest workout. The tail is in nonstop motion. Any muscle that works hard is going to develop deep flavor and character. This is a classic recipe that you can vary by adding some lemon zest or orange peel.

SERVES 4

INGREDIENTS

4 pounds oxtail

Kosher salt

Freshly ground white pepper

½ cup grapeseed or other neutral vegetable oil

1½ cups roughly diced celery root

2 cups roughly diced carrots

2 medium leeks

1 large onion, washed and roughly sliced

4 cloves garlic, whole

1 bunch thyme

½ bunch rosemary

3 cloves

2 bay leaves

8–10 white peppercorns

2 bottles dry red wine

1 pig trotter (or 1 ham hock)

1 tablespoon tomato paste

½ tablespoon flour

———

Preheat the oven to 350 degrees. Season the oxtails with salt and pepper. Heat the oil in a large Dutch oven or braising pan over medium-high heat. Add the oxtails and brown on all sides, about 10 minutes total. Remove and set aside. Add the celery root, carrots, leeks, onion, garlic, thyme, rosemary, cloves, bay leaves, and peppercorns and cook, stirring occasionally, until the vegetables are tender and browned. Add the tomato paste. Mix well, then add the flour and mix again. Deglaze with red wine, scraping up any bits sticking to the pan. Return the oxtails to the pan and add the pig trotter (or ham hock). Bring to a simmer, cover, and braise in the oven until the oxtail is very tender, about 3 hours.

———

Remove the oxtails and trotter from the braising liquid. Set the oxtails aside. Take all the meat off the trotter. Discard the bone and julienne the meat. Strain the braising liquid through a fine sieve, pushing the vegetables through the sieve to give body to the liquid. Return the braising liquid to the pot and bring to a boil. Reduce by one-third over high heat. Degrease (by cooling or skimming) and season with salt and pepper. Gently warm the oxtails in the braising liquid.

PLATING

Serve the meat on a mound of pureed parsnips, polenta, or potatoes, your choice. Surround with the reduced red wine braising liquid. Optional garnish: julienne horseradish.

OUR TASTE NOTES

The meaty bouquet arrives like a salvo of artillery, advancing all the other tastes in a fragrant wave. The onions and garlic follow in its wake, further opening the palate. The meat itself, soft and gelatinous, coats the tongue, smoothing and rounding. The funky side of the meat is pulled out further by the pig trotters. The vinted tang of the braising liquid helps focus the meatiness. Its sugar pushes the sweetness in the vegetables (which are, in turn, pulled by the onions). All that being said, however, this taste starts and ends with meat, big time!

HERBED RABBIT STEW WITH ARTICHOKES AND TOMATOES

RABBIT, LIKE DUCK AND CHICKEN, has two kinds of meat that cook at different rates. The dark meat wants to be cooked long and slow, while the white meat needs less time. This can work to your advantage. The dark meat can be braised leisurely, developing deep layers of flavors. Then, by flash-frying the loins, you get a lovely top note of the meat.

SERVES 4

RABBIT AND SAUCE

2 rabbits, cut up in parts

4 tablespoons flour

Kosher salt

Freshly ground white pepper

2 tablespoons extra virgin olive oil

6 whole cloves garlic

1 cup mixed chopped fresh herbs (oregano, sage, mint, thyme, etc.)

1 cup chicken stock

2 cups chopped, seeded, and peeled tomatoes

2 bay leaves

2 cloves

Pinch sugar

2 tablespoons butter

1 cup chopped basil (reserve for plating)

———

Preheat the oven to 375 degrees. Set the loins aside. Season with salt and pepper. Dust the remaining rabbit with 2 tablespoons of the flour.

———

Heat 1 tablespoon of oil in a large ovenproof skillet over medium-high heat. Add the floured rabbit and the garlic. Brown the rabbit on all sides, about 6 minutes. Add the mixed herbs and continue to cook for another minute. Add the remaining 2 tablespoons of flour and cook, turning the rabbit in the flour, for 1 minute more. Deglaze with chicken stock, scraping up any bits sticking to the pan bottom. Bring the stock to a simmer, then add the tomatoes, bay leaves, and cloves. Cover and braise in the oven until the rabbit is tender, about 1½ hours. Remove the rabbit from the braising liquid and set aside.

———

Strain the braising liquid, pressing the garlic and tomatoes through a medium sieve. Degrease the liquid, then transfer it to a saucepan and bring to a simmer. Season with salt and sugar, then swirl in the butter. Keep the rabbit warm in the sauce over very low heat. Cut the rabbit loins into ½-inch cubes. Season with salt and pepper. Heat the remaining oil in a skillet and pan-roast, tossing the cubes over high heat for 3 minutes.

BRAISED ARTICHOKE STEW

3 tablespoons extra virgin olive oil

1 cup diced onion

2 sprigs rosemary

1 cup roughly diced celery root

6 sprigs thyme

¼ cup parsley, measured then chopped

16 baby artichokes, outer layers removed and bottoms trimmed

1 cup chicken stock

2 cloves garlic, peeled

Juice of ½ lemon

1 cup dry white wine

Kosher salt

Freshly ground white pepper

———

Preheat the oven to 425 degrees. In a lightly oiled sauté pan, over medium-high heat, add the onions, rosemary, celery root, thyme, and parsley and cook until lightly caramelized. Add the artichokes and continue cooking until they begin to brown. Add the chicken stock, garlic, lemon juice, wine, and remaining olive oil. Season with salt and pepper and braise in the oven until the artichokes are tender, about ½ hour.

PLATING

———

Spoon the artichoke stew into four wide soup plates. Arrange a piece of braised rabbit and piece of sautéed on top. Spoon sauce over the rabbit, garnish with chopped basil, and serve.

OUR TASTE NOTES

The floral herbal of the rosemary and thyme accents the salt and meat. Garlic opens the bouquet and brings out the meatiness of the rabbit. The acid lemon and tomato tang pull and brighten the meatiness, while artichokes defuse and soften the strong tastes. After each bite, the herbs come on again. The last note is picante heat.

BRAISED SHORT RIBS OF BEEF WITH AN AROMATIC BARBECUE SAUCE

THIS WAS ONE of the most requested menu items at Lespinasse. Todd Humphries, who later moved on to the Culinary Institute of America, was instrumental in developing it. The tastes in it are huge. Once you commit to one of them, you have upped the ante for all the other tastes. All the tastes are strong here, and any one of them could dominate the dish: therefore you must balance, balance, balance. It took one and a half years to perfect the right ingredients for this recipe, but at this stage of the game, the secret formula is ready to go public. Serve it with pureed parsnips or mashed potatoes. This spice mix is key in adding depth to the sauce. It is essential to grind all spices when you need them. Leftovers may be used next time to coat the meat before sautéing.

SERVES 8

SPICE MIX

1 tablespoon allspice (whole)

1 teaspoon cloves

4 tablespoons coriander seeds

1 bay leaf

1 tablespoon cumin seeds

1 tablespoon Szechuan peppercorns

1 tablespoon black peppercorns

1 tablespoon ground cinnamon

Kosher salt

_____

Toast the allspice, cloves, coriander, bay leaf, cumin, and Szechuan pepper in a dry skillet until fragrant. Add the black peppercorns and grind in a spice grinder or mortar until the mixture is medium fine. Put the spice mix on a plate and add cinnamon and a pinch of salt. Reserve 3 tablespoons for use in the marinade and set the remainder aside.

BRAISING LIQUID

1 cup chopped peeled ginger

3 tablespoons mango pickles (optional; available where Indian condiments are sold)

2 cloves garlic, peeled

1 cup tamarind paste

⅓–½ cup dark brown sugar (to taste, depending on the tanginess of the other ingredients)

3 tablespoons tomato paste

2 cans (28 ounce) tomatoes

5 tablespoons Worcestershire sauce

3 tablespoons spice mix (see above)

4 cups water

_____

Combine all of the ingredients in a food processor and pulse to a smooth paste.

MEAT

8 pounds short ribs (trimmed of excess fat)

Kosher salt

Spice mix (see above)

3 tablespoons corn oil

Braising liquid (see above)

———

Preheat the oven to 350 degrees. Salt the short ribs liberally and dust equally liberally with spice mix. Heat the oil in a large Dutch oven or braising pan over medium-high heat. Add the ribs and brown on all sides, about 6–8 minutes.

———

Bring the braising liquid to a boil in a saucepan then pour it over the ribs. Cover the pan and braise in the oven until the ribs are very tender, about 3 hours. Remove the meat (carefully) from the pan and cover with aluminum foil. Degrease the braising liquid and bring it to a simmer. Season as needed with salt, brown sugar, Worcestershire sauce, and additional spice mix—any leftover spice can be stored in a sealed container for future use. (It is very important to balance the tastes and to season particularly strongly. The recipe will be overly tangy if you don't.)

SAUCE

2 cups braising liquid (see above)

3 tablespoons tarragon, chopped then measured

3 tablespoons parsley, chopped then measured

1 cup Papaya Pickle (page 238), drained, with 2 tablespoons pickling liquid reserved

2 tablespoons butter

Kosher salt

———

Heat the braising liquid over low heat. Add tarragon, parsley, Papaya Pickle and 2 tablespoons pickling liquid, then finish with butter. Add salt to taste and keep warm.

TOPPING

½ cup julienned fresh, peeled horseradish

¼ cup chopped chives

¼ cup celery leaves

1 cup julienned potatoes, crisped in hot oil

PLATING

———

Arrange the ribs on eight warmed plates (preferably on a pureed starchy vegetable—potatoes, turnips, parsnips, whatever you like—short ribs have the breadth of flavor to support the layering of taste upon taste). Spoon the sauce, then the topping over the ribs and serve.

OUR TASTE NOTES

The tangy first notes come from pickles and tomatoes, but most of all from the tamarind. Then meatiness takes over. The aromatic spices pull up more meatiness, while the sweetness in the papaya works with the fruitiness of the tomato to soften the overall tastes. The horseradish contains and punctuates, while its heat continues to push flavor so that all the taste keeps echoing. For such a complex dish, it is striking to us that this flavor analysis is so compact, but that's the way it is, so why complicate things?

THIS WAS ONE OF THOSE invented-while-walking-up-and-down-the-aisles-of-the-super-market dishes; the thought process in it is a good example of how one uses taste elements to design a dish. It was a cold day and the idea of a hearty pork roast conjured up some equally substantial lentils. Then the hard salami and figs suggested themselves for salt and balancing sweetness. We figured the bulbiness of the onions would pull up all of the strong tastes in the wide palate of this recipe. Serve with Lentil Stew (page 181).

SERVES 4

PORK

2 pounds pork loin
Kosher salt
Freshly ground white pepper
2 tablespoons grapeseed or other neutral vegetable oil

_____

Preheat the oven to 350 degrees. Season the pork with salt and pepper. Film a roasting pan with the oil and heat over high heat until it is just about at the smoking point. Sear the pork on all sides until golden, then transfer to the oven and roast, basting frequently with pan juices, until a meat thermometer inserted in the pork indicates a temperature of 160 degrees, about 35 minutes. Remove the pork from the oven and allow it to rest for about 10 minutes. Reserve the pan juices.

TOPPING

2 tablespoons pork pan juices (or extra virgin olive oil)
½ cup finely diced onions
6–8 slices Italian hard salami, julienned
½ cup julienned cornichons
½ pound fresh figs, sliced
Freshly ground white pepper
Pinch sugar

_____

Heat the pan juices (or oil) in a large skillet over medium-high heat. Add the onions and cook, stirring occasionally, until they are golden. Add the hard salami, cornichons, and figs, and continue sautéing for 3 minutes. Season with salt, pepper, and sugar.

PLATING

_____

Slice the pork in 1-inch slices and arrange on warm plates (over the lentils if you are serving them). Spoon the topping over the pork and serve.

The meaty aroma in the pork is accented by the aged, slightly funky bouquet of the hard salami. Its fatty roundness is cut by the tang of the cornichons. The smooth sweetness of the figs calms down the dish, while onions are a background bulby note, which pulls everything up and adds to the sweetness. Sharp saltiness and spiciness are tempered by the starch in the lentils, which have a little bright floral sweetness cooked into them. A meaty bouquet and salt persist at the finish.

OVEN-CRISPED CHICKEN WITH
MAPLE VINEGAR SAUCE

THIS IS A FAST, easy way to make very crisp chicken and *everybody* in the history of humanity loves crispy chicken. Instead of serving it with biscuits and honey, which is traditional in the South, we made it with a maple vinegar sauce, which adds sweetness through maple syrup. We topped it with cranberries, almonds, and shallots, which have the bitterness to cut sweet richness and the nuttiness to work with the maple syrup. Serve with Wilted Endives, Cranberries, and Yams (page 126).

SERVES 4–6

SAUCE

2 tablespoons butter
¼ cup chopped shallots
½ teaspoon cracked black pepper
¼ teaspoon nutmeg
⅓ cup cider vinegar
⅓ cup maple syrup

———

Melt the butter in a medium saucepan over medium-high heat. Add the shallots and cook, stirring occasionally until they are soft and translucent. Add the pepper and nutmeg. Add the vinegar, bring to a boil, then add the maple syrup. Return the sauce to a boil and reduce by half. Set aside.

CHICKEN

1 3- to 4-pound chicken (have butcher splay the chicken, removing the backbone so it lies flat)
Kosher salt
Freshly ground white pepper
2 tablespoons grapeseed or other neutral vegetable oil

———

Preheat the oven to 500 degrees. Make an incision in each of the chicken's thighs, then tuck in the legs. Season the chicken on both sides with salt and pepper.

———

Heat the oil in a large heavy ovenproof skillet over high heat. Place the chicken, skin side down, in the hot pan then immediately transfer it to the oven. After 10 minutes, flip the chicken. Continue roasting, basting every so often, until the thigh juices run clear, 25–30 minutes total roasting. Remove the chicken from the skillet and allow it to rest for about 10 minutes. Pour the fat from the roasting pan and deglaze over medium low with the Maple Vinegar Sauce. Cook just until the sauce pulls together, less than a minute, then set aside in a warm place.

TOPPING

¾ cup slivered almonds

3 tablespoons butter

½ cup dried cranberries

½ cup leeks, finely sliced then measured

1 tablespoon dried homemade bread crumbs

Kosher salt

Freshly ground white pepper

––––––

Combine the almonds and butter in a small skillet. Heat over medium-high heat and cook, turning the almonds frequently, until they are golden brown. Add the cranberries and leeks. Continue pan-roasting for 1 minute. Add the bread crumbs and season with salt and pepper.

PLATING

––––––

Cut the chicken in serving size parts. Arrange the chicken on warm plates. Spoon first sauce, then topping, over the chicken and serve.

OUR TASTE NOTES

First a tangy vinegar aroma and, right along with it, nuttiness from the almonds and butter. The crunchiness from the chicken skin and intense saltiness follow. There's a smooth overall sweetness from the maple syrup, cut by the bitter cranberry and the nuts. The cranberry also has tang, which works with the vinegar to pull out more meaty taste. The flesh of the chicken gives texture and punctuation, plus a full meaty aroma. The end notes are sweet, meaty, and salty.

LADY APPLES WITH GRUYÈRE CELERY PORK POCKETS

THE BEST PORK IS OFTEN fed on apples, so combining them in the pan is just re-introducing two old friends. The prosciutto in the topping and the Gruyère cheese in the stuffing both have an aged funkiness that marries well with the meatiness of pork. The little pockets are a nice way to enjoy the surprise of stuffing without having to go through the process of making a big roast. Sauce with Apple, Mulling Spice, Mustard (page 227). Top with Apple, Brussels Sprout, and Turnip Hash (page 119).

SERVES 4

STUFFED PORK

1 cup finely diced celery

½ cup diced Gruyère cheese

1 tablespoon Dijon mustard

1 teaspoon ground cumin

1 teaspoon kosher salt

Freshly ground white pepper

4 thick pork chops

1 tablespoon grapeseed or other neutral vegetable oil

———

Combine the celery, Gruyère, mustard, and cumin in a bowl. Season with salt and pepper and mix well.

———

Cut a large deep slit along the length of the pork chops, creating a pocket for the stuffing, much like opening a pita. Spoon stuffing into each pocket, then secure with toothpicks.

———

Heat the oil in a large skillet over medium-high heat. Add the pork chops and sauté until golden and cooked through, 4–5 minutes per side. Allow the pork to rest for about 5 minutes.

TOPPING

2 tablespoons butter

1 shallot, finely diced

3 slices prosciutto, diced

½ cup finely diced turnips

Kosher salt

Freshly ground white pepper

Pinch sugar

8 lady apples, peeled, trimmed, cored, and quartered

¼ cup apple cider

Melt the butter in a large skillet over medium-high heat. Add the shallots and prosciutto and cook, stirring occasionally, until the shallots are soft and translucent. Add the turnips, season with salt pepper, and a pinch of sugar, and continue to cook for 3–4 minutes. Add the apples and cook until they are tender, about 3 minutes. Add the apple cider, scraping up any browned bits that have stuck to the pan.

PLATING

Remove the toothpicks from the pork chops and place each on a warm plate. Spoon the topping over the chops and serve.

OUR TASTE NOTES

Sweet, salty, and tangy tastes are delivered at the outset by the topping. Next there is intense meatiness from the pork. The celery is slightly bitter, focusing these broad tastes. The cumin pulls up the funky roundness of the cheese. The fruit mellows the whole dish. The mustard takes the tang of the sauce and carries it over to the sharp side of the cheese, preparing the palate for another round of full tastes.

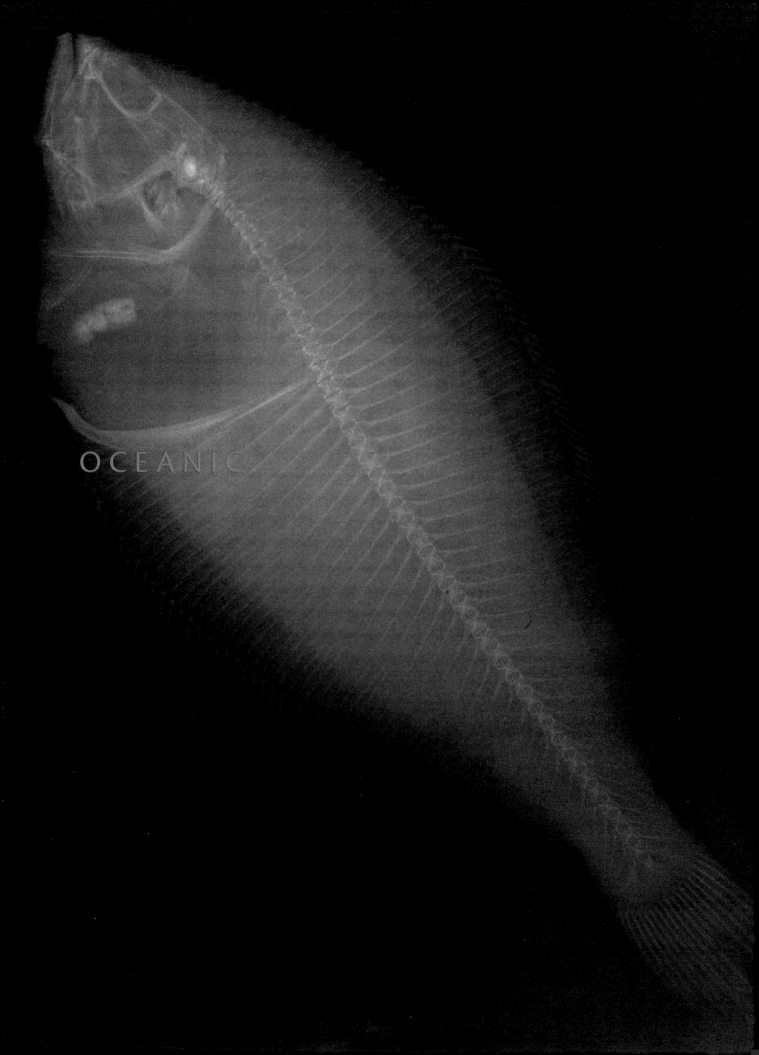

GRILLED SNAPPER FILLET WITH CRISP CAPERS, APRICOTS, AND SHALLOTS

ON THE GULF COAST OF ALABAMA, and all the way around Florida, red snapper is the fish you can usually count on catching a mess of. It's caught elsewhere, but it is southern at heart. Red snapper on a barbecue is one of the most exquisite seafood aromas. When that skin caramelizes on a grill, it is heaven.

SERVES 4

LEMON THYME EMULSION

½ cup dry white wine

1 tablespoon sugar

Juice of ½ lemon

1 tablespoon lemon thyme leaves (or substitute regular thyme)

1 tablespoon extra virgin olive oil

Kosher salt

———

Combine the wine, sugar, lemon juice, and half the thyme leaves in a medium saucepan. Heat over medium heat until the mixture is quite fragrant. Add the oil and beat with an emulsion blender (or a whisk) until frothy. Just before serving, add the remaining thyme, season with salt, beat again, and keep warm.

SPINACH

2 tablespoons extra virgin olive oil

2 cloves garlic, sliced

1 tablespoon finely diced shallot

1 pound spinach, stems removed and chopped

⅓ cup finely diced potato

½ cup chicken stock

Kosher salt

Freshly ground white pepper

Pinch sugar

———

Heat the oil in a skillet over medium-high heat. Add the garlic and shallot and sauté until golden. Add the spinach, a handful at a time, and wilt. Lower heat and add the potatoes, stir once or twice, then add the stock and bring to a simmer. Stir until the potatoes soften and thicken the sauce. Season liberally with salt and pepper then add a touch of sugar. Keep warm.

FISH

1½ pounds snapper fillet, skin on, cut cross-wise across the fillet into 1½-inch strips (if you don't want to do this, even though it looks pretty, the recipe tastes the same if you use a whole uncut fillet)

1 tablespoon corn or other neutral vegetable oil

Kosher salt

Freshly ground white pepper

———

Dry the fillets with paper towels. Brush with oil and grill (over coals if possible), skin side down. When the fish is almost done (it will appear opaque everywhere but the top), flip and briefly sear off the second side. Season the skin side with salt and pepper (don't do this earlier, or the skin will stick to the grating).

TOPPING

2 tablespoons butter

½ cup sliced (raw) almonds

¼ cup small capers

1 cup chopped dried apricots

2 shallots, finely diced

Kosher salt

Freshly ground white pepper

1 tablespoon chopped parsley

———

Melt 1 tablespoon of the butter in a medium skillet over medium heat. Add the almonds and toast, stirring frequently until fragrant and golden. Transfer the almonds to a plate and wipe out the skillet.

———

Add the remaining tablespoon of butter to the pan and heat over medium-high heat. Add the capers and crisp, 2–3 minutes. Return the almonds to the pan, then add the apricots. Sauté until nuts are golden then add the shallots. When the shallots begin to color, season with salt and pepper and add the parsley.

PLATING

———

Mound the spinach on four plates. Arrange the fillets on top. Spoon the topping over the fish, then surround with the emulsion and serve.

The saltiness and tang of the capers hit you first. Hard on their heels, comes the combination of garden and light bitterness in the spinach, the light floral herbal notes in the emulsion. The apricot and almond give texture and a balancing sweetness and roundness. The fish lies smoothly on the palate so that the stronger flavors of the topping and the spinach come through but do not dominate. The herbal emulsion creates a smooth transition from the strong flavors of the topping and vegetable, to the delicate fish. You are left with a light picante heat, and the fresh ocean taste of fish.

SOLE IN CRISPED COUSCOUS, WITH WATERCRESS, GINGER, AND ASPARAGUS BROTH

LEMON SOLE IS A FISH that flakes apart easily. We find it holds up much better if you fry it in a crust. All fish fillets have a thick and thin part, so they tend to cook unevenly. By rolling up fillet strips, as you would a carpet, you get a nice uniform thickness. In addition to gentle handling, the delicacy of the fish demands a broth that is light but not retiring in its tastes. The clean tastes of watercress and ginger go perfectly with freshly caught sole.

SERVES 4

BROTH

2 tablespoons butter

1 medium onion, thinly sliced

½ cup roughly chopped, peeled ginger

1 dozen large asparagus, stalks halved

¾ pound watercress plus ½ cup leaves reserved for garnish

4 cups chicken stock

Kosher salt

1 teaspoon sugar

Cayenne pepper to taste

_____

Melt the butter in a large skillet over medium-high heat. Add the onions and ginger and cook until the onions are translucent. Add the asparagus bottoms (save the tops for garnish—see below), the ¾ pound of watercress, and water or stock. Season with salt and sugar and bring to a simmer. Cook for 20 minutes. Strain the broth through a fine sieve, season with salt, sugar, and cayenne and keep warm over very low heat.

SOLE

4 6-ounce fillets of lemon sole or flounder

½ cup quick-cooking couscous

2 tablespoons grapeseed or other neutral vegetable oil

1 tablespoon butter

Kosher salt

Freshly ground white pepper

_____

Preheat the oven to 300 degrees. Trim the fillets so that you have two straight edges (the fillets will taper toward the tail). Roll each fillet proceeding from the thicker end to the thinner and secure with a toothpick. Dip one end of each roll in couscous.

_____

Heat the oil in a large skillet over medium-high heat. Add the fish, crust side down, and cook until golden, about 3 minutes. Turn the fish, cooking briefly on remaining sides, then transfer the fish to the oven to finish cooking, another 3 minutes.

TOPPING

Asparagus tops (see above)

15 small shrimp

2 tablespoons grapeseed or other neutral oil

¼ cup sliced, peeled ginger

1 shallot, finely chopped

Kosher salt

Freshly ground white pepper

———

Snip off the asparagus florets and set aside. Slice the stems into ½-inch lengths. Blanch both the florets and asparagus lengths in boiling salted water, shock in ice water, then drain.

———

Heat the oil in a skillet over high flame. Toss in the shrimp and ginger. After 1 minute, add the shallots and asparagus. Cook until the shrimp is pink, about 1 minute more.

PLATING

———

Divide the wilted watercress among four soup plates. Place a rolled fillet in each. Spoon the topping over the fish and surround with broth and serve.

OUR TASTE NOTES

The tastes start with two clear aromas: a touch of floral sweetness in the ginger and sweet bulbiness from the shallots and onions. This bouquet pulls up the ocean taste from the shrimp and fish. The grit of the couscous and the light crunch of the asparagus punctuate. There's a sharp, slightly picante edge to the watercress, and light heat from the ginger.

SOFT-SHELL CRABS WITH ORANGE AND BLUE CRAB REMOULADE

SOFT-SHELL CRABS ARE REAL CRABS, but they don't have the deep shellfish flavor of hard-shell crabs. We get that extra layer of flavor in this recipe by making a shellfish sauce with whole hard-shell crabs. The fennel salad on which it is served adds another level of garden crunch and tang that complements the crunchy crust. It may seem wasteful to use whole crabs in the sauce, but that's the only way to get the deep flavor that we're looking for. In classic cuisine, remoulade is mayonnaise with capers, hardboiled eggs, parsley, and cornichon.

SERVES 4 AS AN APPETIZER

REMOULADE

2 cups Basic Lobster Sauce, Crab Variation (page 224)

1 egg yolk, at room temperature

¾ cup grapeseed oil

Kosher salt

Freshly ground white pepper

Cayenne pepper

Zest of 1 orange, very finely diced (reserve juice)

Zest of 1 lime, julienned

———

Bring the sauce to a simmer and reduce by three-fourths. Set aside to cool to room temperature.

———

Combine the cooled stock and egg yolk in a food processor. While processing, drizzle in the oil (small amounts at a time). Process until silky smooth, then season liberally with salt, pepper, and cayenne. Measure 7 tablespoons of the sauce and combine it with half the orange zest and all of the lime zest. Chill the remoulade.

FENNEL SALAD

¼ bulb of fennel, cored and thinly sliced

1 fennel stalk, cut into thin rounds, fronds reserved

Juice of ½ lime

2 tablespoons extra virgin olive oil

Kosher salt

Freshly ground white pepper

Pinch sugar

———

Combine the fennel, rounds of stalk, and fronds in a bowl. Combine the lime juice, reserved orange juice, and oil in a separate bowl, season with salt, pepper, and sugar and set aside.

———

Just before serving, dress the fennel salad with the lime dressing. Toss in orange zest. Season to taste with salt, pepper, and sugar.

STARCHY

MACADAMIA RICE CRÊPE WITH LAYERED VEGETABLES

EVERYBODY, CHEFS INCLUDED, has leftover rice after ordering Chinese takeout. We wanted to make a vegetarian meal with a crispy crêpe as the starting point. Needing something with natural starch to bind it, we tried for macadamia nuts and a whole egg. Making something hot and crisp—and that's what starch is—always pleases even finicky kids. This crêpe batter could easily be used to coat fish or fried quenelles.

SERVES 4

CRÊPE

3 cups cooked white rice

1 egg, lightly beaten

¼ cup milk

½ cup macadamia nuts

½ teaspoon fresh thyme leaves

¼ teaspoon ground nutmeg

¼ tablespoon ground coriander

Kosher salt

½ teaspoon ground white pepper

_____

Combine 1 cup of the rice with the egg, milk, and macadamia nuts in a blender or food processor and puree until almost, but not quite, smooth (about 4 minutes in a food processor). Transfer the mixture to a bowl and stir in the remaining 2 cups of rice. Try out the batter by testing one crêpe in a hot oiled pan. You may find that you need to thin it out and if so, add more milk. Try another crêpe. Readjust. Add the thyme, season with nutmeg, coriander, salt, and pepper and set aside.

VEGETABLES

3 tablespoons grapeseed or other neutral vegetable oil

1 onion, sliced

½ head Chinese cabbage (or savoy), cut into ½-inch cubes

1 beefsteak tomato, sliced

1 medium-sized sweet potato, peeled and shredded

1 tablespoon soy sauce

Juice of 2 lemons

1 cup chopped parsley

Kosher salt

Freshly ground white pepper

Pinch sugar

2 tablespoons butter

¼ cup chopped basil (reserve for garnish)

Heat 2 tablespoons of the oil in a large skillet over medium-high heat. Add the onions and sauté until golden. Add the cabbage, then tomato. Continue cooking until the pan is dry. Add the sweet potato, then the soy sauce and lemon juice. Simmer until the pan is once again dry, then add the parsley, season with salt, pepper, and sugar and swirl in the butter. Remove the vegetables from the heat.

———

Preheat the oven to 400 degrees. Film medium, nonstick, ovenproof skillet with the remaining oil. Spoon half the crêpe mixture into two pancakes in the the pan and cook over low fire. Just as soon as the crêpes begin to set, a minute or two, flip them and crisp the second side. Remove the crêpes to a plate. Make two more crêpes with the remaining batter. When these are lightly golden on both sides, evenly cover them with vegetable mixture then return to the oven and cook for 4–5 minutes. Place the first crêpes on top of the mixture and continue to heat in the oven for 2 minutes.

SAUCE

½ cup soy sauce

¼ cup parsley, chopped

1 tablespoon lemon juice

2 tablespoons sugar

———

Combine all of the ingredients in a bowl and mix well.

PLATING

———

Place the crêpes and vegetable cakes on individual plates. Drizzle sauce around the outside, garnish with basil, and serve.

OUR TASTE NOTES

A crunch from the crêpe is followed by the aromatic spices, which help to bring out the garden vegetables. The lemon and the salt highlight all the other flavors. The macadamia nuts lend a round, creamy, almost buttery note. They also emphasize crispness, which is the fun of this dish.

YELLOW TOMATO COULIS WITH BARLEY, SUMMER HERBS, AND GREEN ZEBRA TOMATOES

BARLEY IS A WONDERFUL, delicately textural grain. But for some reason it is always served with stick-to-your-ribs stuff and only in the dead of winter. Here barley forms the base upon which we built a very subtle and summery soup, relying on textures to keep the flavor transitions going. The different-color tomatoes have different tastes, to be sure, but of equal importance, the colors trigger different associations that affect how you taste. There is surely an emotional subtext to flavor that color draws upon.

SERVES 4 AS AN APPETIZER

SALAD

3 tablespoons extra virgin olive oil

¼ baguette, cut in ½-inch cubes

½ cup cooked barley (best cooked in chicken or vegetable stock)

3 tablespoons sherry vinegar

Kosher salt

Freshly ground white pepper

Pinch sugar

½ cup chopped parsley

1 teaspoon lemon thyme leaves (or regular thyme)

1 teaspoon oregano leaves

1 teaspoon summer savory

2 zebra (or other heirloom) tomatoes, cored, seeded, then julienned

2 tablespoons celery leaves (reserve for garnish)

———

Sauté the bread cubes in 1 tablespoon of the olive oil until golden and crisp, and set aside. Combine the cooked barley, remaining olive oil, and 2 tablespoons of the sherry vinegar in a bowl and season with salt, pepper, and a bit of sugar. Add the herbs and tomatoes.

COULIS

6 medium yellow tomatoes

Kosher salt

Freshly ground white pepper

Pinch sugar

———

Puree the tomatoes then strain through a fine sieve. Season liberally with salt, pepper, and sugar, then chill in a stainless-steel bowl over ice (you have to chill down the tomatoes quickly so they do not render up all of their water). Reseason.

PLATING

Spoon coulis onto four chilled plates. Top with tomato-barley salad, garnish with celery leaves, and serve with croutons.

OUR TASTE NOTES

The garden bouquet of the tomatoes introduces a series of textures. The barley's pastalike toothiness is brightened by the tangy vinegar. The crisp croutons punctuate with crunch while the olive oil accents the light bouquet of the herbs. The celery's crunch and light bitterness focus and punctuate. The coulis is smooth and round, almost as if it were cream or butter. The last note is a nutty starchiness from the barley.

APPLE PAN ROAST WITH STEEL-CUT OATS AND CINNAMON

THIS IS A QUICKIE COBBLER. Serve with vanilla ice cream and maybe a little Calvados in the deglazing. Toasted oats have a unique nuttiness among starches. They crust up well to balance the soft apples and would work nicely with sliced pears and peaches or a new twist on French toast. Yes, this is basically the kind of quick cooking recipe you see on the side of a cereal box, but we tried it and liked it and the kids finished everything.

SERVES 4

INGREDIENTS

1 egg plus 1 yolk, whisked together

¼ cup flour

½ teaspoon kosher salt

½ teaspoon ground black pepper

⅔ cup steel-cut oats (flakes)

½ teaspoon ground cinnamon

5 teaspoons sugar

2 Granny Smiths, peeled, cored, and sliced in ½-inch wedges

2 tablespoons grapeseed or other neutral vegetable oil

Juice of ½ lemon

¼ cup apple cider

2 tablespoons Calvados

2 tablespoons butter

———

Combine the egg and flour. Whisk until smooth, then whisk in ½ teaspoon salt and ¼ teaspoon pepper. Set the binding aside. Mix the oats, cinnamon, and 1 teaspoon sugar together in a bowl. Brush one side of each of the apple wedges with the binding, then dip this side in the oat mixture.

———

Heat the oil in a large skillet over medium heat. Add the apples, crust side down, and cook until the oatmeal is well toasted. Turn the apples over and continue to cook until the apples are tender, about 4 minutes in all.

———

Arrange the apples (like a tarte tatin), crust side up, on a serving plate. Add the remaining sugar to the skillet and allow it to melt and slightly caramelize. Deglaze with a mixture of lemon juice, apple cider, and Calvados. Finish the sauce by swirling in the butter, then pour it over the apples and serve.

OUR TASTE NOTES

The nuttiness of the oats and the spicy aroma of the cinnamon gently pull the sugar forward. The roundness of the butter is cut by the lemon tang and the Calvados.

LENTIL STEW

LENTILS, BY THEMSELVES, are pretty uninspiring. Simply cooked in water, they taste like a Kleenex. Still, if you consider Indian cuisine, it uses green, red, pink, and yellow lentils to great effect. It showers them with a profusion of spices, herbs, and vinegars. These bright, focused ingredients need some nice proletarian brawn to carry them along. Lentils do this deliciously. This dish can be served hot or cold (but if you do serve it cold season forcefully). It also goes well with roasts and game.

SERVES 4 AS A SIDE DISH

INGREDIENTS

1 cup green lentils (Du Puy preferably)

3 tablespoons butter

1 cup thinly sliced onions

1 shallot, thinly sliced

2 cloves garlic, peeled and thinly sliced

1 carrot, peeled and roughly diced

1 cup diced celery root

10 cherry tomatoes (we like Dessert Glory), halved

1 medium-sized leek, washed and sliced in thin rounds

½ cup parsley, measured then roughly chopped

¼ cup dill, measured then roughly chopped

¼ cup fresh oregano leaves

1 tablespoon chopped thyme

1 bay leaf

3 cups chicken stock

Kosher salt

Freshly ground white pepper

———

Soak the lentils overnight. Preheat the oven to 350 degrees. Melt 2 tablespoons of the butter in an ovenproof pot or high-sided skillet over medium-high heat. Add the onions, shallot, garlic, carrot, and celery root and cook until they begin to caramelize, about 5 minutes. Add the lentils, tomatoes, leek, and herbs (saving some herbs for garnish). Add the stock. Bring to a simmer, cover, and bake in the oven, about 25 minutes until the lentils are soft but not mushy. Remove a few tablespoons of the lentils and mash them with a fork or potato masher. Mix the mashed lentils back into the pot with the remaining tablespoon of butter (this will give body to the stew). Season. Top with the reserved fresh herbs and serve.

OUR TASTE NOTES

This is usually a side dish that extends and mellows the robust tastes of stews and roasts. There is an herbal whiff at the outset, followed by sweet tang from the tomatoes and nuttiness from the lentils. The lentils bring out the sweet carrot and the light bitterness of the celery root.

RICE WITH LEMONY HERBS, FAVA BEANS, AND CARAMELIZED PEPPER

SURPRISINGLY, THIS DISH started with a consideration of French-fried potatoes and vinegar. We were struck by the way starch can support tang and, in turn, the way tang cuts starch. Ketchup on fries is the perfect example. Acting on the starch-plus-tangy impulse, we took basmati rice and combined it with lemon-scented herbs, bulby vegetables, and caramelized bell peppers. These are strong, concentrated tastes, but they won't overwhelm the rice. This recipe is a prime example of what we mean when we speak about platforms supporting many tastes. A very versatile side dish.

SERVES 4 AS A SIDE DISH

INGREDIENTS

¼ cup grapeseed or other neutral vegetable oil

1 shallot, thinly sliced

1 clove garlic, thinly sliced

1 cup lemon thyme leaves (or regular thyme with a small amount of lemon zest)

1 cup lemon verbena (the only place you will find this is in your garden or perhaps a local farmers market. Substitute a fragrant basil)

1 tablespoon coriander seeds, toasted

2 cloves

1 bay leaf

1 cup basmati rice

2 cups chicken stock

1 red bell pepper, seeded and julienned

1 pound fava beans, removed from pod, blanched, and shelled

1 tablespoon butter

1 cup parsley leaves

Kosher salt

Freshly ground white pepper

Cayenne pepper

———

Heat half the oil in a large saucepan over medium-high heat. Add the shallots and garlic and cook until translucent. Add the lemon thyme, lemon verbena, coriander seeds, cloves, and bay leaf and cook until fragrant, then add the rice. Cook, stirring, until the rice is translucent, then add the chicken stock and bring to a simmer. Cover the pot, lower the heat, and cook undisturbed until the rice is al dente (8–10 minutes; longer if you prefer it more well done). Remove from the heat.

———

Heat the remaining oil in a skillet over medium-high heat. Add the bell pepper, season with salt and pepper, and cook until the pepper begins to brown, about 3–4 minutes. Add the rice and fava beans. Swirl in the butter, toss in parsley, season liberally with salt, pepper, and cayenne and serve.

OUR TASTE NOTES

It's hard to decide if this dish is about texture or flavor. There's smoothness to the rice, and an almost nutty crunch from the coriander seed and the fava beans. At the same time, there is starchiness to the fava beans that coats the palate. All of this works to counterbalance the combination of bright garden tastes from the bell pepper and the floral and aromatic herbs.

THE ELEMENTS OF CUISINE

THE CHEF'S LARDER

Every great chef resorts to already made stocks, sauces, breadings, etc. to make food that is more interesting and individual. Here are 43 elements of cuisine, mostly made in advance, to create the recipes in this book or to combine in your own creations.

BREADINGS

Breadings are first and foremost crunch. Like a drumroll, they let you know something important is coming in the taste narrative. Breading is a way to punctuate the tastes in toppings and sauces and set them off from the pure taste of the thing that is breaded. But they are far more than just crunch. By including herbs, spices, and seasonings, breadings can be used to foreshadow or complement taste elements that are incorporated more deeply in the main ingredient; for example, through a marinade or braising liquid. Most people have one or two breadings in their repertoire and leave it at that. This leaves a lot off the table. You can combine these breadings with any number of sauces, so feel free to experiment. Obviously you will need a binding element to get the breading to stay on the food. Our basic egg and flour mix which we have used throughout the recipes is our favorite, but you can use buttermilk and flour, milk and flour, and so on. Experiment. If it stays on and stays crisp, it's good.

CORNMEAL, STAR ANISE, AND CLOVES

CORN responds well to anise and cloves which can focus its sweetness. Use this for fish or any white meat (turkey, veal, and so on). We tried it with tautog (blackfish), a fish that Native Americans favored, so it seemed natural to bread it with maize, a native American starch.

MAKES ABOUT 1 CUP

INGREDIENTS

1 tablespoon ground star anise

¾ teaspoon ground cloves

¾ teaspoon kosher salt

¾ teaspoon freshly ground black pepper

1 cup yellow cornmeal

———

Place the star anise and cloves in a dry skillet and toast over medium-low heat until they are fragrant. Grind in a spice grinder or mortar, then add salt, pepper, and cornmeal and mix well.

CREAM OF WHEAT AND CAYENNE

WHEN YOUR "GOURMET" friends hear about this breading they'll say, "Are you kidding? Cream of wheat is baby food!" Just hit this recipe even more powerfully with some cayenne, and see whose palate is grown-up enough for this breading. This is just the thing to coat delicate oysters, scallops, or freshly caught flounder but it can also stand up to thick halibut steaks or salmon fillets. Try it with the Chile Citrus Sauce (page 40).

MAKES ABOUT 1 CUP

INGREDIENTS

¾ teaspoon kosher salt

½ teaspoon cayenne pepper

¾ teaspoon freshly ground white pepper

1 cup cream of wheat

———

Combine all the ingredients and mix well.

PINK LENTIL, TURMERIC, AND GREEN PEPPERCORN

BECAUSE OF ITS COLOR AND TASTE, this breading adds more than simple crunch to a dish. It is extremely versatile, since turmeric is a universal enabler for any spiced aromatic ingredient. The peppercorns have spiced aromatic bouquet, picante heat, and tang. We tested this with shellfish, rabbit loins, chicken breast, and salmon. It always works. Try the Sweet Scallops in a Pink Lentil Crust with a Hot-and-Sweet Bell Pepper Reduction (page 36). It's also very interesting with very thinly sliced eggplant, pumpkin, or butternut squash.

MAKES ABOUT 1 CUP

INGREDIENTS

1 cup pink lentils, ground reasonably fine (about like cornmeal)

2 tablespoons ground turmeric

1 teaspoon kosher salt

2 tablespoons green peppercorns, finely chopped

_____

Mix the lentils, turmeric, and salt together. Just before applying the breading, mix in the peppercorns.

CRISPY RICE FLAKE BREADING

A RICE FLAKE CRUST IS PURE CRISPINESS. The nuttiness of the pan-roasted rice helps pull up flavor in the nose. When you combine this with a sauce with concentrated flavor, it provides a wonderful transition from the strength of the sauce to the full flavor of the main breaded ingredient, such as salmon or flounder. We have tried this breading with fish and chicken served with Grapefruit-Ginger Chutney (p. 243) or Pickled Lemon Confit (page 240). Rice flakes are available in stores specializing in Indian products and often in stores specializing in Oriental ingredients. Sorry, Rice Krispies won't work, and the snap, crackle, and pop are distracting.

MAKES ABOUT 1 CUP

INGREDIENTS

1 cup rice flakes
Kosher salt
Freshly ground white pepper
Pinch cayenne pepper

———

Toss the rice flakes, then season with salt and peppers.

GLAZES

Glazes are most often starters in the taste narrative not finishers. They make a dish look pretty, but they are also a way of delivering a quick flavor message and then leaving the scene and letting other ingredients take over. Sweetness makes a glaze thick and clear and usually calls for a tangy note to balance it out. You may also "glaze things off" by reducing a gelatinous stock; however, the short recipes that follow are start-from-scratch glazes rather than reductions. These glazes will keep for months in the refrigerator (with the exception of the shellfish glaze at the end of this section).

CRANBERRY GLAZE

THIS GLAZE TAKES ADVANTAGE of the fruity, tart, and bitter combination in cranberries. It is spectacular with venison or folded into red cabbage. This combination has sweet fruitiness and tang from the cranberries and port. There is earthy round sweetness from the maple syrup, floral notes from the lemon and orange, and aromatic spices to pull up all these tastes quickly and strongly. Use as a dipping sauce with sautéed chicken breasts, roast turkey, or on a fresh baguette with butter.

INGREDIENTS

½ cup white port
¼ cup maple syrup
Zest of ½ lemon
Zest of ½ orange
4 allspice berries
4 pieces star anise
½ stick cinnamon
Juice of 1½ lemons
2 cups cranberries

──────

Combine ingredients in a saucepan, except for the cranberries. Bring to a boil. Add one cup of cranberries and cook only until the berries pop. Remove cooked berries and repeat with remaining cranberries. Reduce liquid to a thick syrup and return cranberries to the saucepan.

TAMARIND BARBECUE GLAZE

TRADITIONAL AMERICAN BARBECUE SAUCES are of two kinds: vinegar-based and tomato-based. Tomato-based sauces have, sadly, often evolved into a gloppy overly sweet coating. Tamarind, used throughout the Middle East and the Orient, has a great balance of sweetness and tang, and the aromatic spices and ginger we add pull up meaty flavor and give it a kick start. To avoid burning, apply a few minutes before removing the meat from the grill.

GLAZE

1 cup tamarind paste (usually this will be equal to one commercially available package)
2 plum tomatoes, roughly chopped
2 cups water
½ cup roughly chopped fresh ginger
½ cup honey
1 tablespoon ground cumin
1 tablespoon ground coriander seed
Kosher salt

_____

Cut the tamarind into four or five chunks and place in a saucepan with all of the remaining ingredients. Very gently simmer the mixture over low heat, stirring frequently, until the tamarind melts, about 20 minutes. Strain the tamarind mixture through a fine sieve and return it to the pan. Simmer, stirring occasionally, until the mixture has reduced to a syrup. Chill. Adjust seasoning with honey, salt, cumin, and coriander. Refrigerate until needed.

MADEIRA MIRIN GLAZE

ALL THE FLAVOR ELEMENTS in this glaze push taste very powerfully. The Madeira is sweet, but it also has a woody earthiness. The ginger has a floral pull and the tang of the vinegar balances nicely with the sugar for a strong beginning taste. This glaze works brushed over poached fish, sautéed shellfish, steamed bok choy, napa cabbage, or mustard greens.

INGREDIENTS

½ cup Madeira

½ cup soy sauce

1 cup unseasoned rice wine vinegar

½ cup sugar

½ cup finely diced peeled ginger

————

Combine all of the ingredients except 1 tablespoon of the ginger in a saucepan. Bring the mixture to a simmer over medium heat then reduce, stirring occasionally, to a syrup, about 5 minutes. Refrigerate until needed and add the remaining tablespoon of ginger before serving.

THIS IS A VERY STRAIGHT-
FORWARD GLAZE. The heat in
the pepper wakes up taste. The
anise seeds have crunch and the
licorice in them pulls up sweetness. The lemon zest is both floral and slightly tangy, the lemon
juice more so. The honey is both
floral and sweet. Use with any
white meat: chicken, rabbit, or
fish. When chilled, it makes a nice
dressing for steamed asparagus,
grilled fennel, or pan-roasted
artichokes.

INGREDIENTS

Juice of 2 lemons

2½ tablespoons honey

1 teaspoon anise seeds

½ teaspoon cracked black pepper

Zest of ½ lemon, julienned

————

Combine all of the ingredients in a saucepan and bring to a simmer
over medium heat. Reduce, stirring occasionally, until the mixture
has thickened to a syrup consistency, 5–7 minutes. Refrigerate until
needed.

SHELLFISH GLAZE

THIS IS DIFFERENT from our other glazes in that it doesn't rely on sugar or honey as the foundation. Fish and shellfish get an extra-light layer of flavor with this ocean tinged–floral herbal glaze. The shellfish aroma pulls broadly, with bright floral notes from the herbs. There is a hint of sweet and fruit from the tomato and ginger, as well as light tang from the wine and tomato.

INGREDIENTS

2 tablespoons grapeseed or neutral vegetable oil

2 medium shallots, finely sliced

1 tablespoon sliced peeled ginger

1 tablespoon sliced garlic

6 sprigs thyme

1 sprig rosemary

1 bay leaf

2 cloves

Shells and heads of 1 dozen shrimp (or shells from 2 dozen)

½ cup roughly chopped tomato

¼ cup dry white wine

1 cup water

Kosher salt

Freshly ground white pepper

———

Heat the oil in a saucepan over medium-high heat. Add the shallot, ginger, and garlic and cook, stirring occasionally, until they soften and begin to caramelize, about 3 minutes. Add the thyme, then the rosemary, then the bay leaf and cloves. Cook, stirring, until the herbs are fragrant, 1–2 minutes, then add the shrimp shells and heads. Continue cooking, stirring frequently, until the shrimp shells are golden, then add the tomatoes, wine, and water. Bring the mixture to a simmer, scraping up the brown bits that have stuck to the pan, and cook over low heat for about 15 minutes. Strain the broth through a fine sieve then return it to the saucepan and simmer over medium-high heat until reduced by two-thirds. Adjust the seasoning. Refrigerate until needed.

SPICE MIXES

Spice mixes most often sit on the outside of a platform food such as meat, fish, poultry, and vegetables. They have a strong bouquet and pull out floral, fruity, sweet, bitter, and bulby notes at the beginning and end of the taste. They don't infuse the main ingredient, so they don't over-whelm delicate flavors. They are a way of adding power without permeating a dish. Also, they allow you to add an echoing layer to spices that might be cooked into a deep flavor layer of a sauce or stock. In most of our spice mixes, the dried spices are pan-roasted and then ground. Roasting releases the volatile oils in the spices. Oils, like fat, carry flavor over the palate. These mixes, with the exception of the Yogurt Mix (page 202), can be made in advance and stored for weeks but, since they are so easy to prepare, we prefer to make them as needed.

SHELLFISH SPICE MIX

THE FENNEL HAS A LICORICE ELEMENT to it that pulls up sweetness. The cloves sharpen and focus tastes and also pull up sweetness. The rosemary is floral herbal, and pulls out delicate oceanic tones from shellfish. Dust on the outside of shrimp, scallops, or fish before sautéing, baking, or grilling.

INGREDIENTS

4 teaspoons fennel seed
½ bay leaf
3 cloves
1 teaspoon fresh rosemary leaves

_____

Combine the fennel, bay leaf, and cloves in a small dry skillet and toast over medium heat until fragrant. Transfer to a spice grinder or mortar, add the rosemary leaves, and grind medium fine.

ANCHO CARDAMOM SPICE MIX

CARDAMOM IS VERY POWERFUL and it focuses aromas. Coriander seeds tempers cardamom, and the star anise pulls up sweetness. The ancho chili adds smoky picante heat, and the salt pushes everything else. Use with grilled or baked fish and vegetable kebabs.

INGREDIENTS

1 tablespoon coriander seed
1 piece star anise
1 tablespoon cardamom seed
1 teaspoon ground ancho chili
1 teaspoon kosher salt

_____

Combine the coriander, star anise, and cardamom in a small dry skillet and toast over medium heat until fragrant. Transfer to a spice grinder or mortar and grind medium fine. Add the ancho powder and salt and mix well.

YOGURT SPICE MIX

THIS IS INSPIRED by the use of spices and yogurt in Indian cuisine. Floyd Cardoz was instrumental in developing many of these spice mixes. Cardamom's aromatic bouquet complements citrus. Cinnamon pulls up sweetness, which helps to accent fruitiness. Mace has spiced aromatic tones that complement a wide spectrum of flavors, as does the cumin in a more focused way. The yogurt rounds but also pushes with its slight acid tang. We have served this with steak tartare, cold roast lamb or chicken, grilled zucchini, fennel, and vegetable kebabs. You probably should call this a sauce or condiment, but it is so filled with aromatic spices and the flavor it delivers is so spice based, we think of it whenever we think of spice mixes.

INGREDIENTS

1 cinnamon stick

1 teaspoon ground mace

½ teaspoon green cardamom seeds

1 teaspoon cumin seeds

½ teaspoon black peppercorns

1 cup yogurt

2 tablespoons lemon juice

¼ teaspoon kosher salt

¼ teaspoon sugar

_____

Combine the mace, cardamom, cumin, and peppercorns in a small dry skillet and toast over medium heat until fragrant. Transfer to a spice grinder or mortar and grind medium fine. Mix with the yogurt, add lemon juice, and season with salt and sugar. Serve chilled.

GAME SPICE MIX

MEAT IS THE MOST ROBUST PLATFORM in terms of bouquet and texture. It wants spices that punctuate and focus, that pull out accents and notes. The coriander seed and juniper have floral notes. Cumin and allspice give roundness and breadth to the mix. The pepper, of course, pushes all the other flavors through picante heat. Beef is well suited to this mix, and gamier meats such as venison or wild duck work beautifully as well.

INGREDIENTS

½ tablespoon allspice berries

2 tablespoons coriander seed

½ teaspoon cumin seed

1 tablespoon juniper berries

1 teaspoon black peppercorns

————

Combine the allspice, coriander, cumin, juniper berries, and peppercorns in a small dry skillet and toast over medium heat until fragrant. Transfer to a spice grinder or mortar and grind medium fine.

ORANGE SPICE MIX

DUCK, PHEASANT, AND PORK ROAST all have an affinity for orange. The floral citrus top notes come forward ahead of the gaminess. They charm the palate, while the funky game taste works on a subliminal level. The anise pulls up sweetness from the meat, while the clove pulls savory notes and rounds the bouquet.

INGREDIENTS

2 pieces star anise

2 cloves

½ teaspoon Szechuan peppercorns

3 tablespoons ground dried orange peel (to do this, zest an orange and leave it on a plate for a day to dry out, or put in low oven, 180 degrees, for two hours, then grind)

———

Combine the star anise, cloves, and Szechuan peppercorns in a small dry skillet and toast over medium heat until fragrant. Transfer to a spice grinder or mortar and grind medium fine. Add the ground orange peel and mix well.

TOPPINGS

The crisp skin of a chicken or grilled fish, or the charred outside of a chop or steak, is an inviting challenge to the chef. The food does not want to arrive naked on your plate. Toppings have instant, pleasing texture, which is usually in the form of crunch. As with glazes, they can provide a means to deliver concentrated flavor without overwhelming more subtle and delicate ingredients. Often a topping will combine every fundamental taste (sweet, tangy, salty, picante) and almost as often, some floral herbal notes. It is the first thing you taste, stating the themes that are cooked more deeply into the food. Toppings are an element of cuisine glossed over in cooking literature, but they are the inventive chef's real "go-to" item: every palate loves toppings, and just about every dish should have one.

ONION, HORSERADISH, APPLE

THE ONIONS ARE THERE TO OPEN and pull up flavor, especially the sweetness of the apple. The horseradish gives crunch and sharpness to punctuate. The mustard, too, has sharpness but with tang as well to pull out deeper flavors. This combination works well with gamier meats — cutting fattiness and pulling deeper layers of flavor. Serve with braised cabbage, pork chops, sausages, and pheasant.

4 SERVINGS

TOPPING

2 tablespoons corn oil

2 apples, peeled, cored, and cut into eighths

½ teaspoon sugar

½ pound pearl onions, blanched 3–4 minutes

2 tablespoons butter

2 tablespoons freshly grated horseradish

1 tablespoon Dijon mustard

½ cup chopped parsley

———

Film a large skillet with half the oil and heat over medium-high heat. Add the apples and sugar and cook, turning the apples occasionally, until they are tender and golden. Set the apples aside and wipe out the pan.

———

Film the skillet with the remaining oil, heat over medium-high heat, and add the onions. Cook, stirring occasionally, until the onions are tender and lightly browned, about 5 minutes. Add the apples and the butter to the onions and cook, swirling the pan as the butter melts, for about 1 minute. Add the mustard and horseradish and heat through. Toss with parsley just before serving.

BABY ARTICHOKES WITH CASHEW, LEMON ZEST, AND CHIVES

THIS TOPPING HAS ENOUGH SUBSTANCE for it to be served as a vegetable dish in its own right. However, since it is so dry in texture and defined in its component tastes, it works well with wet dishes like Striped Bass with Caramelized Scallions in Green Peppercorn Citrus Sauce (page 38). Artichokes roasted in this way are nutty and round tasting.

MAKES ABOUT 4 CUPS

INGREDIENTS

6 baby artichokes
3 tablespoons extra virgin olive oil
Kosher salt
¼ cup chopped cashews, toasted
Zest of 3 lemons, julienned
¼ cup chopped chives

———

Pull away the tough outer leaves from the baby artichokes. Trim the stems, cut off the tops of the leaves, and quarter the artichokes (babies do not have any furry chokes). As you work, sqeeze lemon juice over the trimmed artichokes to preserve their flavor. Place them in a large skillet with the oil and heat over medium-high heat. Season with salt and cook, turning the artichokes in the oil, until they are tender and golden, at least 8 minutes. Add the cashews, reduce the heat to low, and cook until the artichokes are fork tender, 2–3 minutes. Add the lemon zest and chives. Remove from heat and serve.

STEAMED FISH, ALL ON ITS OWN, can be a little flaccid; it often needs something to wake up flavor. The lemon and orange zest have light texture and a floral bouquet that pulls up flavor. The tang is good counterpoint to the ocean taste of fish. Chives, like shallots, open the nose, and they also sharpen and punctuate. This topping would also work as a *gremolata* for many fish stews.

4 SERVINGS

INGREDIENTS

1 tablespoon extra virgin olive oil

2 tablespoons diced shallots

1 tablespoon butter

½ tablespoon diced orange zest

½ tablespoon diced lemon zest

1 tablespoon chopped chives

Kosher salt

Freshly ground white pepper

———

Heat the oil in a small skillet over medium-high heat. Add the shallots and cook, stirring occasionally, until they begin to brown. Add the butter and citrus zests and cook until the topping gives off a fruity aroma. Add the chives and salt and pepper and serve.

SPICED AROMATIC ELEMENTS pull up the fragrant notes in any broiled meat. The shallots open the bouquet and the mint pulls up sweetness. The mustard seeds have crunch that punctuates and a little sharpness that closes down the broad meatiness of the main ingredient being garnished.

SERVES 4

INGREDIENTS

2 teaspoons extra virgin olive oil

⅓ cup pignoli nuts

1 teaspoon finely diced shallots

½ teaspoon mustard seeds

½ teaspoon ajowan (or cumin) seeds

½ teaspoon curry powder

1 tablespoon dried homemade bread crumbs

Kosher salt

Freshly ground white pepper

1 teaspoon julienned mint

————

Heat the oil in a small skillet over medium-high heat. Add the pignoli nuts and toast until lightly golden. Add the shallots, then mustard seed, ajowan, and curry powder. Continue toasting until the mixture is fragrant. Add the bread crumbs, toast lightly, then season with salt and pepper. Toss with mint before serving.

TARO JULIENNE WITH CILANTRO AND JICAMA

ALTHOUGH MANY OF OUR TOPPINGS combine all the basic push tastes — salt, tang, heat, sweetness — this topping is more focused, spotlighting garden flavors, adding crunch, and using floral herbal elements. The jicama is especially crunchy and fruity. Serve with a soft, smooth vegetable dish like summer squash or eggplant. Serve fresh garden topping for broiled fish or chicken or flank steak.

SERVES 4

INGREDIENTS

⅓ cup corn or other neutral oil

½ cup julienne of taro

½ tablespoon julienned peeled ginger

⅓ cup Thai basil (you may substitute regular basil)

1 tablespoon diced red bell pepper

1 teaspoon diced jicama

1 tablespoon chopped cilantro

Pinch of kosher salt

_____

Heat oil in a small saucepan over medium heat until it is hot but not yet smoking. Add the taro and deep fry, until golden and crunchy, about 3 minutes. Drain the taro on paper towels. Just before serving, toss the taro with the ginger, basil, pepper, jicama, and cilantro. Season with salt and serve.

HUCKLEBERRY CHIVE BUTTER
WITH PECANS

THIS STARTED OUT AS
SOMETHING to serve with foie
gras. It is simultaneously sweet
and tangy to offset the rich
meatiness. It begins with buttery
roundness, followed by the fruitiness and tang of the huckleberries. The pecans are nutty and
crunchy, as are the sunflower
seeds. The shallots pull up all the
broad aroma of the ingredients.
This is terrific with lamb chops,
pork, venison, duck confit, and
game birds such as woodcock,
grouse, or braised duck legs.

SERVES 4

INGREDIENTS

½ tablespoon butter

1 tablespoon chopped pecans

1 tablespoon chopped sunflower seeds

1 shallot, chopped

2 tablespoons huckleberries or blueberries

1 tablespoon finely diced yams

Kosher salt

Freshly ground white pepper

———

Melt the butter in a medium skillet over medium heat. Add the
pecans and sunflower seeds and pan-roast until fragrant. When
they begin to color, add the shallot. Cook, stirring occasionally, for
2 minutes. Remove the topping from the heat and, just before
serving, add the huckleberries and yams and season with salt and
pepper.

A MAGICAL COMBINATION inspired by the way Sicilians combine fruits and bulby vegetables with salty and tangy elements such as anchovies or capers. There is a North African feel to this, as there is with much Sicilian and Spanish food — no surprise given their proximity to North Africa and the centuries they were ruled by the Moors. This is absolutely foolproof with any grilled fish fillet.

INGREDIENTS

2 tablespoons extra virgin olive oil
1 tablespoon capers (brined or salted), drained
1 tablespoon chopped shallots
1 teaspoon chopped golden raisins
Zest of ½ lemon

———

Heat the oil in a skillet over medium-high heat. Dry the capers then add them to the pan. Crisp the capers, then remove them with a slotted spoon and drain on paper towels. Add the shallots and raisins to the skillet and cook, stirring occasionally, until the shallots are nicely browned. Return the crisped capers to the pan, toss with lemon zest, and serve.

BROTHS

Broths and bouillons are the gentler, less complex cousins of sauces. They rely on a few clear flavors. There is something attractive about clear stocks — they seem to have a nutritionally moral aspect. Maybe it's because grandmothers are associated with beef bouillons and chicken stocks. We won't reprise basic meat and poultry stocks here — there are more than enough books that do that. These are more unusual flavor combinations. You can easily see any garnishes that are added into broths and bouillons and this visual element enhances the whole experience.

THIS IS A LIGHT, but not retiring broth. If you bread and fry things in the modern style — that is, crisping one side only — then you can serve chicken or fish, crisp side up, and surround it with this broth, which will cut the saltiness of many breadings. You may garnish with chervil, basil, or chives, to introduce a floral herbal top note.

SERVES 4

INGREDIENTS

1 tablespoon butter

¼ cup finely diced shallots

½ cup finely diced butternut squash

1 cup dry white wine

2 tablespoons honey

3–4 teaspoons lemon juice

Kosher salt

Freshly ground white pepper

———

Melt butter in a medium saucepan over medium-high heat. Add the shallots and cook, stirring occasionally, until they are golden. Add the squash, wine, honey, and lemon juice. Adjust the seasoning with salt, pepper, and lemon juice and serve.

TOMATO FENNEL BROTH

A BRACINGLY BRIGHT BROTH.
The licorice of the fennel and
Pernod pulls out sweetness, while
the tomato adds brightness and
light tang, which is concentrated
by the lemon. In warm weather,
this is a refreshing dressing on
grilled vegetables, fish, or shellfish.

SERVES 4

INGREDIENTS

2 tablespoons extra virgin olive oil

1 cup chopped fennel bulb (save fennel trimmings)

1 tablespoon fennel seeds

2 tablespoons Pernod or anisette

2 cups homemade chicken stock

Kosher salt

Freshly ground white pepper

Pinch cayenne pepper

Pinch sugar

1 lemon, ½ zested and juiced, and ½ sectioned

2 tablespoons finely diced tomato

―――――

Film a saucepan with the olive oil and heat over medium heat. Add
the chopped fennel and cook, stirring occasionally, for 3–4 minutes.
Add the fennel seeds and lightly toast. Deglaze the pan with half
the Pernod. When the pan is almost dry, add the stock. Simmer the
mixture for 8–10 minutes, then strain through a fine sieve. Return
the broth to the pan and season with salt, pepper, cayenne, and
sugar. Add the remaining Pernod, lemon sections, juice, and zest.
Just before serving add the tomato to the bouillon. Garnish with
I tablespoon of fennel "hair" (the tiny leaves at the end of the bulb).
Serve warm.

ALMOND MILK BROTH

THIS DISH is a creamy New England seafood chowder. To it we added the magical combination of brown butter, almonds, and nutmeg. It brings an element of nutty woodiness to the combination that marries splendidly with a crisp Chardonnay. The white flesh of a light fish looks so beautiful with this broth that you'd think fish was designed to be served with it. You could also try it with hash brown potatoes, very crisp.

SERVES 4

INGREDIENTS

2 tablespoons butter
½ cup sliced almonds
½ teaspoon grated nutmeg
½ teaspoon flour
2 cups milk
Kosher salt
Freshly ground white pepper
Pinch cayenne pepper
⅓ cup slivered leeks

_____

Melt the butter in a medium saucepan over medium-high heat. Add the almonds and toast until golden. Stir in the nutmeg, then the flour. Add the milk and, stirring frequently, bring to a boil; the liquid thickens slightly. Lower the heat and season well with salt, pepper, and cayenne, then, just before serving, add the slivered leeks. Serve warm.

SAUCES

The beauty of sauce is in the power and depth of taste. Sauces are almost always reduced strongly, which means you have to season and reseason constantly to get the right balance. Sauces are more melded and deeply layered than the other elements in the chef's larder. They often include some oil or butterfat to help round and diffuse tastes. Sauces are the deep voice that harmonizes with the lighter notes of toppings or spice mixes. In the classic repertoire, sauces are the basis of cuisine. Generations of mediocre restaurants have obscured their errors in preparation and second-rate ingredients behind showy sauces. That's kind of like hoping that lots of makeup will undo decades of partying too hard. Still, a true sign of talent in the kitchen is the ability to make good sauces.

BASIC RED WINE SAUCE

THIS IS AN EXTREMELY POWERFUL SAUCE. It needs that power to do its job in creating an overall flavor for the strong presence of meat in a dish. The main element is vinted tang — fruity and astringent. The butter softens this and the sugar, in like manner, balances the tannic bitterness of the concentrated red wine. Remember, the more you reduce red wine, the more you will need to counteract bitter with sweet. The bulby vegetables add bouquet and sweetness, which will pull flavor out of the main ingredient. The celery root adds some complementary, but softened, bitterness and focus.

SERVES 4

INGREDIENTS

2 tablespoons grapeseed or other neutral oil
½ cup chopped carrots
½ cup chopped celery root
½ cup chopped onion
1 shallot, roughly chopped
1 clove garlic, sliced
1 bottle dry red wine
3–4 tablespoons butter
Kosher salt
Freshly ground black pepper
2–3 tablespoons sugar
Dash of brandy

———

Heat the oil in a medium saucepan over medium heat. Add the carrots, celery root, onions, shallot, and garlic and cook, turning them occasionally, until tender and browned, about 15 minutes. Add the wine and bring to a boil, scraping up any browned bits that have stuck to the pan. Reduce by two-thirds, then strain through a fine sieve. Return the sauce to the pan and reduce again until the sauce coats the back of a wooden spoon. Just before serving, swirl the butter into the warm sauce off the heat. Season with salt, pepper, and sugar. When the taste is balanced, add the brandy. Set aside.

———

VENISON VARIATION: Follow the steps for the Basic Red Wine Sauce as above but add 1 teaspoon of juniper berries and about a teaspoon of cracked black pepper to the vegetables when they are almost caramelized. Add the wine, reduce, strain, and reduce again as above but finish the sauce with ¼ cup of gin in place of the brandy. Reserve the vegetables to use as a delicious topping.

———

LOBSTER VARIATION: Gather your ingredients as for the Basic Red Wine Sauce but cut all the vegetables in paysanne style — small thin cubes about ¼ inch. Proceed as in the basic sauce but don't strain before adding the butter. The neatly cut vegetables remain in the finished sauce.

ROSE CHAMPAGNE EMULSION

THE PERFECT KICK-START for a fish dish. We went for pink champagne just for color and appearance. The lemon adds tang, the emulsion adds roundness and flavor, without adding more fat. The chives focus the taste. The shallots pull out the sweetness and fruitiness of grape and lemon. Salt, pepper, cayenne, and sugar are fundamental push tastes that boost overall flavor. Use with grilled or steamed white-fleshed fish.

SERVES 4

INGREDIENTS

2 tablespoons finely diced shallots

1½ cups pink champagne

3 tablespoons butter

Kosher salt

Freshly ground white pepper

Cayenne pepper

Pinch sugar

Lemon juice (to taste)

¼ cup chive lengths (about ½ inch)

_____

Combine the shallots and champagne in a medium saucepan and bring to a boil. Reduce by three-fourths, then lower the heat to a simmer and whisk in the butter. Season with salt, pepper, cayenne, and sugar. Balance with lemon juice. Just before serving, beat with an emulsion blender (or whisk vigorously). Add the chives and serve warm.

FLORAL HERBAL AIOLI

AIOLI, OR GARLIC MAYON-NAISE, is a classic Mediterranean garnish, most notably in bouillabaisse. Adding herbs and aromatic spices introduces greater definition to the smoothness of mayonnaise. After all, aioli is simply mayonnaise plus the bulbiness of garlic. We went a little bit further with herbs and spices.

SERVES 4

INGREDIENTS

2 heads garlic

⅓ cup extra virgin olive oil

1 tablespoon white wine or lemon juice

½ teaspoon curry powder

½ teaspoon ground coriander seed

½ teaspoon ground cumin

Pinch sugar

Pinch cayenne pepper

Freshly ground white pepper

Kosher salt

¼ cup coriander leaves measured then chopped

———

Roast the heads of garlic until deep golden brown, about 1 hour at 325 degrees. Remove the softened garlic from the skins and mash in a bowl. Whisk in the oil. Add the wine, spices, sugar, peppers, salt, and chopped coriander.

BASIC LOBSTER SAUCE

THIS IS A BASIC SAUCE that is often glossed over or ignored in other books — maybe because it can be sloppy to prepare. Two pieces of advice: be neater, or don't mind the mess. The resulting sauce is absolutely fundamental to so many shellfish and fish-based dishes that to ignore it would be like cooking without heating.

MAKES ABOUT 3 CUPS

INGREDIENTS

3 lobster shells (you may use the shells from raw or cooked lobsters)

½ cup extra virgin olive oil

1 cup chopped celery

1 cup roughly chopped onions

1 cup roughly chopped carrots

1 head of garlic, split in half

1 cup roughly chopped celery root

4 sprigs thyme

1 sprig rosemary

1 cup roughly chopped tomatoes

1 tablespoon tomato paste

¼ cup cognac

1 quart water

2 large cloves, sliced

Kosher salt

Freshly ground white pepper

Pinch cayenne pepper

2 tablespoons butter

———

Pound or chop the lobster shells into small pieces, then grind to a paste with 3 tablespoons of the oil in a mortar or food processor.

———

Heat 2 tablespoons of the oil over medium heat in a large pot. Add the celery, onions, carrots, garlic, and celery root and cook until they begin to brown. Then add the thyme and rosemary. Add the lobster-shell paste and cook, for 4–5 minutes, scraping up bits as they stick. Add the tomatoes and tomato paste, and a pinch of salt and cook 4–5 minutes. Deglaze with cognac, then add the water and simmer for 15–20 minutes. Strain the lobster stock through a fine strainer. Return to the pot and reduce by one-third. Shortly before serving, add the remaining 3 tablespoons of oil and the butter and beat with an immersion blender (or whisk vigorously). Season with salt, pepper, cayenne, and a dash of brandy.

———

CRAB VARIATION. Substitute 4 quartered blue crab shells for the lobster shells. Proceed as above but do not add the final 3 tablespoons of oil and do not beat.

CLEAN AND BRIGHT. Chili oil and green peppercorns are picante with spiced aromatic notes. There is a floral herbal bouquet as well as tang to the lemon. The tarragon, with its licoricey notes, pulls up floral and sweet aspects in the ingredient being sauced. It will work well with delicate striped bass, sturgeon, halibut, or cod because the cleanness and brightness of tang and heat feels like the ocean on a sunny day.

MAKES ABOUT 1 CUP

INGREDIENTS

1 cup lemon juice

Zest of ½ lemon

3 tablespoons honey

3 tablespoons green peppercorns

2 tablespoons extra virgin olive oil

Chinese chili oil (to taste)

Kosher salt

⅓ cup roughly chopped tarragon

———

Combine the lemon juice, zest, and honey in a medium saucepan. Warm over medium heat. Crush peppercorns and add them to the sauce. Stir in olive oil, a drop of chili oil, and 2 pinches of salt. Just before serving, add tarragon.

KUNZ KETJAP

THIS SAUCE WAS ORIGINALLY MADE at Lespinasse with Steak Tartare (page 142), but it is also a wonderful alternative to standard shrimp cocktail sauce, or as a coating for grilled fish. It includes aromatic spices that the Indonesians put in a sauce they call kecap manis, and, along with them, the ingredients used in steak tartare. The result is one of the strongest combinations of flavors in this book. Feel free to use it anyplace you have the urge for ketchup. That way you can satisfy your basic ketchup urge with something that sounds a little more gourmetish.

MAKES ABOUT ½ CUP

INGREDIENTS

¼ cup tomato ketchup

1 tablespoon kecap manis (sweet Indonesian soy sauce — you may substitute regular soy sauce with ½ teaspoon sugar)

1 tablespoon red wine vinegar

1 tablespoon honey mustard

½ teaspoon Tabasco sauce

1 teaspoon curry powder

1 teaspoon ground cumin

Juice of 1 lemon

¼ teaspoon kosher salt

———

Combine all the ingredients in a mixing bowl, whisk, and refrigerate for at least 1 hour. Serve chilled or at room temperature. Will keep in the refrigerator for two days.

APPLE, MULLING SPICE, MUSTARD

A VERY SIMPLE THEORY

HERE: Apple and mulling spices work so well together. The combination of sweet fruitiness and aromatic spices cuts the fattiness and heaviness in main ingredients. By adding mustard, which has oil, tang, and salt, it gets the body that makes it a true sauce. Serve with Lady Apples with Gruyère Celery Pork Pockets (page 158), fresh or smoked ham, or venison.

SERVES 4

INGREDIENTS

1 cup apple skins and cores

1 cup apple juice

½ lemon, quartered

1 stick cinnamon

8 allspice berries

4 cloves

2 tablespoons grainy mustard

1 tablespoon butter

———

Combine all of the ingredients except the mustard and butter in a medium saucepan and bring to a simmer over medium-high heat. Simmer for 10–12 minutes, then strain through a fine strainer. Return the sauce to the pan and reduce by half. Add the mustard and butter and beat with an emulsion blender (or whisk vigorously). Serve warm.

GINGER CURRY SAUCE

BASICALLY A LIGHT MAY-ONNAISE, with floral herbal and spiced aromatic notes. The curry and ginger, both aromatic, pull out garden flavor in grilled vegetables. The white wine and lemon add good brightening tang. This sauce works well with cold poached fish, or as a dipping sauce for wontons or ravioli.

ABOUT 1 CUP

INGREDIENTS

¼ cup white wine
1 tablespoon finely diced shallots
1 teaspoon curry powder
1 egg yolk
½ cup corn or other neutral vegetable oil
1 tablespoon grated peeled ginger
Juice of ½ lemon
Kosher salt
Freshly ground white pepper
¼ cup chopped celery leaf

———

Combine the white wine, shallots, and curry in a medium saucepan and bring to a simmer. Reduce by half, then cool to room temperature. (You can do this quickly by placing the mixture in a stainless-steel mixing bowl and placing that bowl in a larger, ice-filled bowl.) Whisk in the egg yolk, then, still whisking, slowly add the oil. Add the grated ginger and the lemon juice. Season with salt and pepper and, just before serving, fold in the chopped celery leaf. Refrigerate until needed.

AROMATIC MUSTARD SAUCE

A SIMPLE LAST-MINUTE SAUCE that goes with game, cabbage, bitter greens, braised or smoked pork. The mustard focuses and punctuates while adding light sweetness. The cumin pulls up meaty notes, and the shallots also pull out meat and sweetness. The celery gives crunch and a light bitter focus.

MAKES ABOUT 1 CUP

INGREDIENTS

2 shallots, finely diced

2 cups dry white wine

2 teaspoons cumin seeds

2 tablespoons butter

2 tablespoons grainy mustard

Kosher salt

Freshly ground white pepper

⅔ cup finely diced celery root

———

Combine the shallots, wine, and cumin in a medium saucepan and bring to a simmer. Reduce by half (the sauce can be made in advance up to this point, then reheated and finished just before serving). Swirl in the butter and mustard, season with salt and pepper and beat with an emulsion blender (or whisk vigorously). Add the celery root and keep warm over very low heat.

BRINES

Because they rely on the most potent push taste—salt—brines infuse whatever is put into them with powerful flavors. This is the opposite of what you try to accomplish with glazes, which give a coating of powerful tastes, without taking over the deeper flavors of the foods to which they are applied. You will always need to balance brines with tang and possibly sweetness.

JUNIPER GAME BRINE

IN THE WILD, game and juniper have a natural affinity for one another: deer, grouse, and turkey eat juniper berries all fall. Gin is made with juniper berries, so it is a nice medium to carry that flavor. The floral and spiced aromatic notes of the juniper will pull flavor from the flesh of the game. The pepper will, likewise, push all the taste elements. Maple syrup sweetens and thereby softens the sharp edges of this combination. There is also a slight bitter edge to the pepper and caramelized sugar that cuts saltiness. Its sweetness works with the peppery heat to push flavor forward. Use it with all kinds of game. For more layers of flavor, coat the game with Game Spice Mix (page 203).

MAKES ABOUT 2¼ CUPS

INGREDIENTS

1 cup gin

1¼ tablespoons cracked black pepper

2 tablespoons ground juniper berries

1¼ tablespoons sea salt

1¼ cups maple syrup

————

Combine all the ingredients and whisk. Refrigerate until needed.

THE FIRST TIME WE TRIED these ingredients, they left us flat — a lot of separate flavors, but no unity to produce something new. Putting the ingredients in a food processor changed that. It was both new and packed a lot of punch. The taste begins with the floral bouquet of lemon, which is reinforced on the palate by the floral element in the olives. These olives and salt are cut somewhat by the tang of the lemon. Sugar pushes the fruitiness of the lemon. This is a recipe that cries out for something sweetly tart to balance it. When we served it with sautéed boneless chicken breasts, it was wonderful with our Cranberry Glaze (page 194) as a dipping sauce. This is a very good brine for infusing veal, chicken, or delicate shellfish such as scallops.

MAKES ABOUT 2 CUPS

INGREDIENTS

2 lemons, zest chopped and juice reserved

1 tablespoon chopped fresh sage

¼ cup Madeira

1½ tablespoons coarse salt

⅓ cup extra virgin olive oil

2 tablespoons sugar

1 tablespoon pitted chopped niçoise or kalamata olives

———

Combine all the ingredients in a food processor and blend until smooth. Refrigerate until needed.

BOURBON MUSTARD BRINE

IN THINKING ABOUT PORK AND BRINING, the rich redness of goulash provided an inspiration. Whiskey suggested itself as a strong medium for infusing flavor and carrying the salt into the meat. Its barrel woodiness imparts smokiness. Paprika — even hot paprika — will always have a softening effect on competing assertive flavors. The mustard has sharpness and tang to cut strong tastes. Pheasant or rabbit works well with this.

MAKES ABOUT 2¼ CUPS

INGREDIENTS

1 cup whiskey

¼ cup coarse salt

½ cup Dijon mustard

4 teaspoons paprika

½ cup honey

———

Combine the ingredients. Mix well then refrigerate until needed.

PICKLES

Pickles are the essence of tanginess. Whether it is vinegar, lemon juice, or some other tangy element, the acid in pickles stimulates the palate and makes it receptive to other flavors. Although not every pickle is crunchy, the second element to pickles is usually the crunchy texture that punctuates each group of tastes in every mouthful. We haven't given serving amounts here because basically we make a bunch of pickles and keep them in the refrigerator until ready to use. These amounts are easily good for a number of meals.

CRANBERRIES POACHED IN SPICED PORT AND LEMON

CRANBERRY SAUCE IS OFTEN TOO MUSHY. We wanted something that gave the tang and bite of cranberry sauce, while preserving the substance of the fruit. It gets additional balance of fruit from the citrus. The allspice and anise work, as they do in baking, to pull out sweetness to balance the strong tang and light bitterness in the cranberry.

INGREDIENTS

⅓ cup port
1½ cups fresh orange juice
2 tablespoons honey
Zest of ½ lemon
Zest of ½ orange
1 teaspoon ground allspice
2 pieces star anise
1 stick cinnamon
¾ pound cranberries

———

Combine all of the ingredients, except the cranberries, in a saucepan and bring to boil. Separate the cranberries into two batches and poach them each in the boiling liquid. (After twenty seconds you should hear the skins begin to pop.) Remove cranberries from the liquid with slotted spoon and set aside.

———

Reduce the liquid by half, pour it over the cranberries. Serve, or refrigerate until needed.

PAPAYA PICKLE

THIS PICKLE HAS A SOFT-
NESS to it that melds well with
long-braised meats. The spices
are ones that we use to pan-roast
short ribs that we serve with a
tamarind barbecue sauce. Like
meat, papaya has a funkiness to
it, so it makes sense that the
pickle includes the same spices
that work for meat. Use with any
grilled meat, or as a pick-me-up
for a summer green salad.

INGREDIENTS

2 cups distilled white vinegar

1 cup sugar

Zest of 2 lemons

2 cups thinly sliced papaya (2 smallish papaya)

1 tablespoon short rib spice mix (page 151)

——————

Bring the vinegar and sugar to a boil in a small saucepan. Add the zest. Toss the papaya with the spice mix. Pour the vinegar mixture over the papaya and refrigerate until needed.

PICKLED LEMON CONFIT

SARIG, AN ISRAELI CHEF at
Lespinasse, created this recipe.
You will find preserved and pickled lemon recipes throughout the
Mideast and across southern Asia
and India. There is really no clear
progression of tastes here, just
extremely concentrated flavor.
The big elements are fruity tang,
sweetness, the heat of the
pepper, and strong spiced aromatic and floral herbal. It works
well with grilled fish or in salads.
It is particularly effective in moist
toppings with nuts, shallots, dried
tomatoes, olives, herbs, etc. Nice
with roast fowl, for example our
Poached and Crisped Turkey Leg
Provençale (page 110).

INGREDIENTS

10 lemons, halved and seeded (as best you can)

1 stick cinnamon

2 bay leaves

1 teaspoon allspice (whole)

1 tablespoon coriander seeds

1 tablespoon white peppercorns

3 cups water

¼ teaspoon turmeric

1 jalapeño pepper

¼ cup sugar

10 sprigs thyme

———

Combine all the ingredients in a saucepan and bring to a boil, then
cool. Repeat, boiling and cooling four or five times until the lemons
are almost translucent. Put the lemons in a glass jar, cover with confit liquid, and store in the refrigerator until needed.

ONION MARMALADE

IN THE GENERAL CATEGORY of chutneys and confits, which are all-purpose flavor enhancers, this is one of the most versatile. It doesn't get more bulby than this. Made with red wine, it can hold its own with venison and red cabbage. For fish or fowl, substitute white wine and white vinegar in the recipe. For sweetening, maple syrup works as well as honey. For a change on the classic summer salad of sliced raw onions and tomatoes, try this onion marmalade with some gnarly beefsteak tomatoes.

INGREDIENTS

3 large white onions, thinly sliced
1 cup red wine vinegar
4 cups dry red wine
6 tablespoons honey
Kosher salt
Freshly ground white pepper

———

Combine the onions, red wine, vinegar, and half the honey in a saucepan and bring to a boil over high heat. Add salt and reduce by half, then turn heat down to medium (you want a steady simmer). Continue reducing until the onions are very soft and the pan is almost dry. Balance with salt, pepper, a dash of vinegar, and, depending on how sweet the onions are, the rest of the honey. Don't be afraid of making the tastes too strong. That is almost impossible. Be aggressive. Underline that last point if you are serving this with cold vegetables because cold versions of a highly flavored recipe always require even more aggressive seasoning. Serve warm or at room temperature.

PICKLED RAMPS

COMPARED TO THE RIPE SWEETNESS of summer fruits and vegetables, ramps have the sharp insistence of a crying baby. This recipe makes a virtue of that sharpness — a quality that all bulby vegetables have but one that we usually cook away. The sharpness of the ramps punctuates and focuses taste. The bulbiness pulls up a wide bouquet, while the spiced aromatic notes of the coriander and fennel focus tastes. The sugar and the licorice-flavor fennel round and soften. For an intense meat such as pork, it cuts right through it, pulls flavor, and sets you up for the next bite. Treat it as one of a number of tapas with an aperitif. Toss it into a green salad.

INGREDIENTS

1 pound early spring ramps
1 cup cider vinegar
½ cup sugar
1 cinnamon stick
1 bay leaf
1 dried hot pepper
1 tablespoon coriander seeds
½ tablespoon fennel seeds

———

Trim the green tops from the ramps. Wash. Split any large ramps lengthwise. Blanch all the ramps for 15 seconds in boiling salted water. Shock them in ice water, drain, and dry. Combine the vinegar and sugar in a saucepan and bring to a boil. Place the ramps in a large jar. Add spices, then pour hot vinegar mixture over the ramps. Seal the jars and let cool to room temperature overnight. Refrigerate until needed. (Save any leftover pickling juice for vinaigrette, mayonnaise, sandwiches, cole slaw, and salads.)

GRAPEFRUIT—GINGER CHUTNEY

WE MADE THIS RECIPE with sugar first and then elected to go with honey: in addition to a sweet push, the honey also exerts a floral pull that helps to smooth the transition from powerful tanginess and chili heat to the main ingredient in the recipe (fish one time, braised duck leg another). This chutney is quite good with smoked turkey, duck, or pork loin, even smoked mozzarella for an appetizer. Pita stuffed with grilled eggplant and pepper gets a really good kick with this. Experiment.

INGREDIENTS

1 tablespoon sugar

2 grapefruits, peeled, sectioned, and juice reserved

½ small dried Chinese chili

3 tablespoons honey

Zest of ½ orange, julienned

1 tablespoon lemon juice

1 tablespoon onion seeds (optional)

1½ tablespoons finely diced ginger

Kosher salt

Freshly ground white pepper

————

Combine the sugar, grapefruit, chili, and honey in a saucepan and bring to a boil. Reduce until it looks like there is more fruit than liquid, then add orange zest, lemon juice, onion seeds (if used), and ginger. Season with salt and pepper.

GINGER CONFIT

THIS RECIPE IS BUILT around the floral and picante components of ginger, pushed by the sweet floral notes of the honey. Cloves and cinnamon also add focus and pull up tastes, while the crunchy bulby onion seeds figure in the initial bouquet. The vermouth and lemon juice complement the fruitiness of the ginger. Serve with shrimp, lobster, steamed bok choy, watercress, or spinach. In other words, use to balance bitter or as an enlivening condiment.

INGREDIENTS

½ cup julienned peeled ginger
½ cup white vermouth
3 tablespoons honey
6 cloves
1 stick cinnamon
Juice of 1 lemon
Juice of 1 lime
Zest of 1 lemon, julienned
1 dried Chinese chili
1 teaspoon onion seeds
Kosher salt
Freshly ground white pepper

————

Combine all the ingredients in a saucepan except the onion seeds, salt, and pepper and reduce to a jamlike consistency by simmering over medium-high heat. Cool to room temperature. Add the onion seeds and season with salt and pepper.

A CHEF'S NOTE

I FIRST SAW *THE SOUND OF MUSIC* IN SINGAPORE. I was eight years old. My parents took my two brothers and me to the cinema off Orchard Road. I loved the film. It was my first look at Switzerland, my father's native land, a place I had never seen. It was so far off and exotic. We left the theater and walked through a street market. My mom, a brunette Irishwoman with a passion for decorating, painting, and interesting food, stopped at a market stall and got us pork from a Chinese vendor. It was pressed so thin you could almost see through it. It was barbecued with fragrant spices. I remember biting into it and tasting sweetness and the aroma of ground spices (although I couldn't identify the ingredients at the time). Something happened inside me. I loved the taste of that simple pork in the same way that I loved the songs that I had just heard Julie Andrews and her movie family sing for us. To me, that taste *was* music.

I was beginning to learn the language of taste. My next strong food memory is about a year later. An Indian man, next to my father's silver-plating shop, made chapati — a kind of thin bread. He used his own mix of spices every day as he worked over his little outdoor stove. The way he handled and flipped and pressed the dough reminded me of a circus juggler. To me, the technique and the taste were inseparable.

Often in those years my brothers and I would join my dad for an afternoon's fishing. Sometimes we would even catch fish! Grass carp, and little fish whose names we never knew, but which we would bring home and give to our gardener, who would grill them up with yet another mix of freshly ground ingredients from the spice stalls. By the time I was ten years old, my brothers and I knew and loved the spices and tastes of Asia. Then came a big change for our family as we pulled up stakes and moved across the globe to Switzerland. I felt cold air for the first time. I saw snow for the first time. It looked impossible and magical and wonderful.

They say that people learn languages most easily when they're young. With that move to Switzerland I began as a young boy to learn whole new languages of taste. Where many Europeans go to the East to discover new and exotic flavors, I found the flavors of Bern, my

Swiss canton, as exotic as *The Tales of the Arabian Nights*. The cheeses with their aroma and textures captivated me. The smell of the cooking oils of Asia was replaced by the sweet and nutty bouquet of butter. Spaghetti and meat sauce, a food that every child who has ever tasted has loved instantly, was, for the Kunz brothers, adoration at first slurp.

There was fresh cream from cows that pastured in the mountains — so thick and sweet. I had my first Swiss chocolate — creamy, satiny, sweet, with just a hint of bitter. And then there was all that meat! In Asia meat is almost — not quite, but almost — served as parsimoniously as truffles are in Europe: kind of an extra treat, rarely the main ingredient. In Switzerland, we had beef cheeks and roasts of pork, beef, and lamb. And there was wine, which I learned about as an ingredient long before I fell in love with it as a beverage. It was as varied and sensual as the endlessly stimulating tropical fruits of Asia. I truly doubt I would have become a chef, and certainly would not have become the kind of chef that I am, if I had not had the opportunity to learn rich new contrasting tastes at that young age.

I was hooked on taste and food. I decided to make it my life. Or maybe it would be better to say that love of food made the decision for me and I just went where my inner chef told me to go. I kept tasting. As a student in Bern, my apprentice friends and I would spend whatever extra money we had — which was not much — eating. We particularly loved *Bernerplatte*, huge platters of pig ears, tongue, and smoked pork loin with braised green beans. If that Indian man who made those chapatis next to Dad's shop had seen us devouring these forbidden foods, he would surely have thought we were emissaries of Kali the Destroyer.

Then I met a young Swiss girl, from Lausanne, and we fell in love, and her parents fell in love with a soup that I purloined from the kitchen of the Beau Rivage (where I was working). Twenty-five years later they still praise that mussel soup that I made in my first years in a kitchen. That's pretty good for in-laws. Nicole shared my passion for exploring new tastes, and we would ramble through the woods and hills around Lausanne, where I had become a wild mushroom fancier. One afternoon we were in the Alps. The day started warm and we climbed higher. The weather turned cold, all of a sudden, and it began to snow heavily. Just then, we came upon a patch of porcini mushrooms, perfectly ripe. They were golden and brown with an inch of snow on their caps. Had we found them two hours later, they would have been ruined by the cold. Nicole and I took them home and prepared them with cream as white as that snow. They became another word in my new language of tastes, one that was refined in the kitchen of Freddy Girardet in Crissier.

Next, East met West and Old met New when I took a job at Restaurant Plume in the Regent Hotel in Hong Kong. To my newly learned culinary techniques I added my taste memories of Asia. Every new idea I had in my four years in Hong Kong seemed to be a new incarnation of a childhood memory. Alone among my Western colleagues I became the first *gwailo* (non-Chinese) chef to shop extensively in the rich open-air markets. I started to cook with durrian, mangosteen, lichees — fruits so intense that I am sure that the day after God created them he decided not to publicize them because once exposed to them, people might spend all day eating fruit instead of working and praying. One of my desserts, chilled soup of jasmine blossoms with caramel-stuffed lichees, was so popular that people would book tables at our pricey restaurant just to have that dessert. Most often it was young couples in love — about to get married. Who knows? I might have stumbled on a secret love potion.

When work brought us to New York, it was a blizzard of new tastes. No other city in the world has such variety of food: bagels, pizza, felafel, corned beef on rye, dim sum, sushi, Jamaican jerk chicken, Korean barbecue, Cuban pressed sandwiches, Guatemalan tamales . . . even homemade chapati. My taste vocabulary grew and grew. It was an embarrassment of riches that required some deep thinking if I was ever to bring order out of that delicious chaos.

Gradually, I learned to *speak* a taste language, but it was something that happened over time, lots of cooking, and lots of tasting. What I did first was to *absorb* it in an instinctual way. I understood taste the way a blues musician can improvise and feel music but often cannot write it down and analyze it like a classically trained musician. It wasn't until a writer friend, Peter Kaminsky, and I began to talk one afternoon while trout fishing on the banks of the Esopus Creek in the Catskills that I realized although I knew and he knew what taste is, we didn't have a common vocabulary to express that knowledge. Still, we found we communicated easily. We talked about mushrooms, rainbow trout, New York restaurants, our kids, chef's knives, and July heat waves. The next spring, we returned to the Catskills with our families to prepare a meal of food that we foraged or caught: eel, shad roe, cattail hearts, milkweed, wild ramps, morels, chamomile, lamb's-quarters, wild strawberries. More new tastes for me. Peter and I have continued to cook, write, and think about taste in the years since.

I haven't finished learning the language of taste, that inner language that we all understand before we speak it. But I feel that now is as good a time as any to try and put the language into words.

GRAY KUNZ

ACKNOWLEDGMENTS

Thanks to Freddy Girardet for his counsel, art, and encouragement.
To Bob Burns and Rudi Greiner, who brought a young chef to Hong
Kong and set him free to combine the cuisines of Europe and the Far
East. To Todd Humphries, Floyd Cardoz, Rocco Dispirito, John Rellah,
Sammy DeMarco, David Cunningham, Troy Dupuy, Chris Broberg,
Michael Klug, Jill Rose, Frank Fung, Andrew Carmellini, Dan Budd,
Eric Bedoucha, Larry Finn, Naj Zouhari, Helga Mayr, Julie Pryce, Nick
Oltarsh, Jon Mathieson, and Robert Curren who turned a chef's inspi-
rations into great restaurant dining. Peter Tishman for giving birth to
Lespinasse. Rich Segal at the St. Regis. Tony Fortuna for his flair and
courtliness in running it day-to-day. To all the wait staff, sommeliers,
busboys, hostesses, stewards, potwashers, and runners, without whom
there are no great restaurants. To every concierge and doorman, too.
And the purveyors: farmers, fishermen, and ranchers. To Pierre and
Elianne Henchoz, the Beau-Rivage Palace in Lausanne, the Baur Au Lac
in Zürich, the Parc-des-Eaux-Vives in Geneva, the Regent Hotel in Hong
Kong, and the Peninsula in New York. Vivian Holtzman and Cathy
Young for their attention to detail. Mark Reiter for his appetite and
counsel. Dawn Drzal for getting our weird idea, Sarah Crichton for
believing in it, and our editor, Deborah Baker, for her patience, support,
and appetite.

To Alfred and Moira, Shaughn and Kevin Kunz — a family
that created a love for food. To Alfred and Rita Mingard, and their son
Francis who welcomed a chef into the family and shared some secret
mushroom spots. To Lena Gottlieb and Geraldine Kaminsky, for their
keen sense of onions, Dana Cowin for helping to make a complex
thing simpler, Bryan Miller for getting us together for the cup of coffee
that led to this book, Cher Lewis for her home, friendship, and taste-
buds, Josh Feigenbaum for his beach house even if it didn't have fish,
Paul Dixon for 10 pounds of North Carolina shrimp. For Babu, the
spice man who made the most memorable grinds in Singapore, and
Ah Soon and Ah Yee, two nannies in that town whose skill in the
kitchen introduced the Kunz kids to the elements of taste.

INDEX

(Page numbers in *italic* refer to illustrations.)